W9-DGM-549

MESOPOTAMIA

VOLUME 5

MESOPOTAMIA

Copenhagen Studies in Assyriology
VOLUME 5

THE ARCHITECTURE OF IRAQ IN THE THIRD MILLENNIUM B.C.

by HARRIET E.W. CRAWFORD
Sometime Calouste Gulbenkian Research Fellow
Lucy Cavendish College, Cambridge

AKADEMISK FORLAG
Copenhagen 1977

The publication of this book
has been made possible
by a generous grant from
THE MARC FITCH FUND

© Akademisk Forlag &
Harriet E.W. Crawford 1977
ISBN 87–500–1703–9
Printed by: J.J.Trykteknik A/S
Copenhagen

NA220
.C89
1977
SWTS

CONTENTS

FIGURES

PREFACE

This catalogue of the architectural evidence from Mesopotamia is envisaged as the first step in an attempt to reconstruct a social and economic history of the third millennium in this area. Information recovered from field surveys on settlement patterns and settlement types, documentary sources, representational art and the evidence of the buildings themselves have all been used. Even so there are many gaps in the record, but it is hoped that it will be useful to students to find the existing material tabulated in concise form instead of scattered through nineteenth century travellers' tales and inaccessible periodicals. Features of importance for dating purposes are isolated and an attempt is made to study the micro-settlement patterns, in the few instances where enough data is available to make this possible. One or two tentative sociological conclusions are drawn; the lacunae in the evidence are underlined and some specific problems are suggested as urgently needing solution by excavation and further research.

It is with great pleasure that I acknowledge the help I received from Lucy Cavendish College in the three years in which I held a research fellowship there; the friendship and support of members of the college have been invaluable. The college has also contributed towards the cost of producing this monograph. I am grateful to Dr P.R.S.Moorey for his most helpful criticisms of the manuscript; to Mrs Rowe who deciphered and typed the original draft and to Mo Robinson who drew the plans. Finally I would like to express my gratitude to Professor Laessøe and the Assyriological Institute, University of Copenhagen for producing this monograph and to the following for permission to reproduce plans of which they hold the copyright: University of Chicago Press; Professor and Dr Moortgat; Professor A.Parrot; University of Pennsylvania Press; Dr J.Reade.

Cambridge, Harriet Crawford. December 1975.

ABBREVIATIONS

Abbreviations used other than those in the standard list compiled by "Iraq".

C.A.H.   Cambridge Ancient History. Third edition.

G.M.A.   P.Amiet. Glyptique Mésopotamienne Archaique. Paris 1961.

M.A.M.   Mission archaéologique de Mari.

P.F.D.   P.Delougaz. Pottery from the Diyala. Chicago 1952.

P.H.D.   P.Delougaz, H.Hill, & S.Lloyd. Private houses and graves from the Diyala. Chicago 1967.

P.S.T.   P.Delougaz and S.Lloyd. Pre-Sargonid temples in the Diyala region. Chicago 1942.

S.F.D.   H.Frankfort. Stratified cylinder seals from the Diyala region. Chicago 1955.

S.A.O.C.   Studies in ancient oriental civilization. Chicago.

CHAPTER I

It is an anomaly, though an understandable one in terms of expediency, that the presence of any historical data tends to retard the collection of purely archaeological evidence and to minimise its importance; a sad situation when the aims of both disciplines are the same and when their evidence is very often complementary. The Early Dynastic period is the first in Mesopotamia for which there is any historical documentation, but in order to obtain even a fragmented picture of the period the documentary evidence must be considered in conjunction with the archaeological sources. The modern academic tendency towards rigid specialisation is not helpful towards this dual approach to the reconstruction of the past, and indeed runs counter to the current movement in archaeology which is in effect towards a multiple rather than a dual approach; it embraces the study of the environment, the ecology, the physical anthropology as well as the linguistics, philology and history where these are available. Such a complex approach demanding much specialist knowledge cannot be undertaken by a single individual but rather by a team. One of the earliest examples of this inter-disciplinary approach is provided by the survey of the Jarmo region edited by Braidwood[1] and shows what can be achieved with evidence that thirty years ago no-one would have troubled to collect or study.

If one attempts to apply this inter-disciplinary approach to a study of the third millennium it is perhaps logical to start with a description of the environment, for it can be argued that the rest of the evidence is conditioned to a greater or lesser extent by this. Until man could control his environment adequately by the development of technology the environment was the deciding factor in his cultural development and indeed remains an important and sometimes decisive one throughout the history of the world. The political unit now known as Iraq is not a geographical one,[2] in fact it consists of several very disparate zones ranging from the temperate uplands and fertile intramontane valleys, which were the political centre of the Assyrian Empire round cities like Nineveh and Khorsabad, through river valleys such as the Diyala, via the great silt plains of ancient Akkad and Sumer, virtually desert away from the river banks, to the boggy marshes of the Shatt-el-Arab and the Persian Gulf. It has been fairly well established that no major land movements or climatic changes have taken place in the Holocene period but the movements of the Persian Gulf coastline are still the subject of discussion. Lees and Falcon's contention that the head of the Gulf had remained more or less static has recently been disputed by C.E.Larsen in an article which claims that there was a considerable rise in sea level between the years 7,000–4,000 B.C. with the head of the Gulf coming up as far as the Hor-al-Hammar. The encroachment of swamps about the year 2,000 B.C. was noted by Adams and Nissen in their survey of the Uruk region and at an earlier period such a rise in sea level might be the explanation for the flood level observed at Ur. In the present state of our knowledge Larsen's evidence carries a great deal of weight. Other environmental changes, many caused directly or indirectly by man, have occurred and have important consequences. Two of the most far-reaching of these have been the desiccation and consequent erosion caused by over-grazing and deforestation in the upland areas, and the sterility and depopulation of the irrigated areas, particularly ancient Sumer, caused by salinization of the soil.[3] Paradoxically the deposition of silt in large quantities on the alluvial plain has tended to preserve the status quo as the land is sinking at a rate sufficient to compensate for the deposition of hundreds of cubic feet of silt a year; the recent survey of the Warka region by Adams and Nissen has shown that the picture is more diverse in this particular area than had hitherto been supposed. The amount of silt deposited varied between eight and two metres. Adams also stresses the importance of wind erosion and deposition in the formation of today's landscape.[4] The silt has made it difficult to trace the remains of early agriculture and the courses of secondary canals, but the different courses of the Tigris and the Euphrates and the courses of the most important canals can be plotted with a fair degree of certainty. It is noticeable that the settlements cluster along the waterways thus emphasising their importance in the shaping of the political geography of the country and its economy. In the early periods little attempt was made to improve on the natural network of small streams; most of the labour seems to have been directed to diking the water into the fields from the streams and in keeping the streams themselves running freely. The cultivated land was confined to a strip on either side of the streams which could be easily watered by these simple methods. Gradually a tendency develops towards improving fewer, larger channels as the number of settlements decreases and the size of the remaining ones increases. Adams's survey has underlined the dangers of generalising from the particular and he is reluctant to make general statements about the process of urbanization which appears to have varied considerably from area to area. It is, of course, possible to argue that sedimentation, erosion and redeposition have made retrieval of the information needed for such a study virtually impossible. However, the broad outline of the picture indicates a development from widely and evenly spaced settlements of similar size, to a smaller number of clustered settlements and finaly in some areas to a hierarchical grouping of sites. There are indications that this process may be earliest in the Nippur area, but by the Jemdet Nasr period it is attested round Kish and Uruk as well.[5]

There are, broadly speaking, two main zones in Iraq, the Northern hilly broken area, where irrigation was used, but was not an essential prerequisite of agriculture, and the southern alluvium, potentially very fertile, entirely dependant on irrigation, and between the natural resources of the two areas. The north had access to wood and stone as well as agricultural produce, wheat, barley, flax etc., orchard produce and a supply of wild game; in the south there were no adequate supplies of raw materials, the date palm is the main supply of poor quality wood; fish replaced game as the main supply of wild protein; barley was the staple cereal; mud and reeds the main building materials. It has been argued elsewhere that it is this very poverty of resources which led to the development of the first urban communities in the south rather than in the north.[6]

It will be seen that it is not possible to talk about Iraq as a unit in prehistoric times and indeed at many periods the north and south provide interesting contrasts in their rate of development and in the direction of that development. The two geographical areas do not exactly reflect political boundaries and raise certain problems of terminology. The terms Sumer and Akkad, Babylonia and Assyria are not entirely satisfactory as they all carry political overtones; north and south Iraq are usually taken to imply the area north or south of Baghdad and this again fails to reflect the physical division of the country which runs on a line from Hit to Samarra. The provinces of the Arabs[7] most nearly reflect this physical dichotomy, the Jazirah lying a little further north than the geological line just mentioned and Iraq lying between it and the Persian Gulf. The use of the name Iraq for this limited area would only confuse matters further so a compromise is suggested; the north will be referred to as the Jazirah and the south as Southern Iraq. The north, or Jazirah, is geographically and culturally closer to Anatolia and Syria than the south, while the south tends to look south and east for its foreign relations, although the Euphrates is a notable highway to the north and west at all times. It is hoped to bring out these contrasts as well as the obvious links between the two areas in the subsequent chapters.

There is a strong case to be made out for the presence in Mesopotamia by the Early Dynastic period of three linguistically differentiated peoples, but we cannot tell today whether these linguistic differences reflect true racial differences. It is usually assumed that there was a pre-Sumerian population, whose existence is suggested by the presence of non-Sumerian and non-Semitic place names and words from the earliest periods for which we have evidence.[8] The archaeological evidence does not offer any help in identifying the remains of the pre-Sumerian people. If the period at which the Sumerians entered Southern Iraq could be finally established we might then be able to collate the remains of the pre-Sumerians.

The Sumerians are often supposed to have moved into Mesopotamia from the east,[9] in the Ubaid period but it should be remembered that a journey from the east to west across Southern Iraq is geographically more of an obstacle race than one from south to north and that the Euphrates is navigable where the Tigris is not. The discovery of Ubaid sites on the west side of the Persian Gulf has raised the possibility that the Ubaid people might have entered Mesopotamia from the south, from the Persian Gulf and perhaps the Iranian coast.[10] This does not rule out an Iranian origin for them. If one accepts that the Ubaid people were Sumerian and one supposes this southern point of entry it perhaps explains the cluster of early, and incidentally sacred Sumerian settlements in the south and their clustering on the navigable stream of the Euphrates river. The course of the river would be the obvious route for these incomers to follow and this supposition would also go some way to explaining why the bulk of the Sumerian population seems to have settled in the south of Iraq although they must have penetrated in some numbers up the river to Mari and perhaps as far as Tell Chuera in Syria.[11]

In the present state of our knowledge it is extremely difficult to determine the extent of the Sumerian presence at Mari. A rapid review of the excavated material leaves no doubt as to the cultural dominance of the Sumerians,[12] architecture, statuary, costume and religious practice all bear witness to it. However, this could be explained in any number of ways from close economic and cultural contacts, perhaps reinforced by colonies of Sumerian specialists e.g. merchants and craftsmen in Mari, to the presence of a large Sumerian element in the indigenous population. It seems very unlikely to be the result of conquest by one of the Sumerian city states. By the time we have our earliest inscriptions from the Mari the rulers appear to bear Semitic names, but Sumerian names appear on several of the votive statues. One of the best known is that of Ur-Nanse, the temple singer. Sumerian ideograms are also quite widely used in the Pre-Sargonid inscriptions. The statues, with Semitic inscriptions, represent people who appear indistinguishable physically from their Sumerian counterparts in the south. It is an interesting problem and one which is unfortunately unlikely to be solved.[13]

The thesis that the Sumerians entered Mesopotamia at the beginning of the Ubaid period is by no means universally accepted. A strong case for their entry during the Uruk period can also be made. It is not necessary to equate the entry of new peoples into a land, far from overpopulated, with strife and destruction. The gradual amalgamation of elements of diverse origins with a local population is well attested in later periods and it may well be a process such as this which produced the Sumerian civilization. This realization casts some doubts on the validity of the "continuity of culture" argument as ably put forward by Frankfort and Seton Lloyd.

If the Sumerian period and Sumerian culture are seen as the result of an amalgam of traditions and traits, some indigenous and some foreign, the identification of any one group ceases to be of paramount importance. The fact that some architectural features survive from Eridu VI up till the beginning of the third millennium does not mean that the Sumerians had to be the builders of Eridu VI.[14] They may have arrived much later and assimilated the religious mores of the "pre-Sumerians" or may possibly have had similar religious habits in their country of origin.

The Sumerian element in the population was traditionally regarded as conservative, the Semitic Akkadians, on the other hand, being regarded as lively and virile, credited for example with the introduction of life and vigour into the artistic repertoire of the Sargonid Period.[15] It must not be forgotten, however, that if we accept the suggestion that the Sumerians were already in the country at the beginning of the protoliterate period they may be held responsible for the superb naturalistic art of the Uruk Period. Some scholars now reasonably argue that it is not possible to isolate Sumerian traits on the one hand and Semitic ones on the other in the art of the third millennium.

The Semitic speaking element in the population, the bulk of it settling in the Jazirah, is usually accepted as coming from nomadic elements in the West.[16] The recruiting of mercenaries from among the Semitic tribesmen was a considerable factor in the urbanising of the nomads and the gradual infiltration of nomadic peoples into the settled areas is a phenomenon well known to the present day. The Semitic speakers are not, however, to be regarded as culturally unsophisticated. By E.D. III we find statues in the classic Sumerian style with Semitic inscriptions and the king lists show the presence of rulers and officials with Semitic names in several major Sumerian cities.[17] Perhaps the situation in Mesopotamia at the beginning of the Early Dynastic period was in some ways analagous to the situation in England during the Anglo-Saxon invasions. The indigeneous population, already a fairly mixed bag, probably of diverse origins, was a prey to raids from marauding neighbours who in some cases decided to settle and as a result became partially assimilated into the local population to whose culture they contributed new and lively elements.[18] Some of these invaders came in to Britain as Laeti or mercenaries under the last phase of Roman occupation just as the Semitic tribesmen in Sumer came in as Sumerian mercenaries. The assimilation in Sumer probably never became total as new peoples were infiltrating all the time, a process which continues into modern times. The view of some authorities such as J.Van Dijk[19] that the Akkadian period saw an all-out religious and racial war in which the Sumerian priesthood of Nippur allied itself with the Gutians to bring about the downfall of Semitic Akkad, seems unlikely on present evidence. Would the passionately Sumerian Third Dynasty of Ur have allowed offerings to be made to a divine Semitic Naram-Sin if this religious struggle had been in progress only a comparatively short time previously? The archaeological evidence also argues strongly against any such violent reaction and indicates a process of largely peaceful absorption and readjustment. There is some evidence in historic times for the movement of people back to the desert in conditions of political stress. This may have been the case in the Agade period when Adams has shown a considerable fall in the number of settlement sites, without a comparable increase in size in the remaining ones.[21]

In Southern Iraq, field surveys are making it increasingly plain that settlements were clustered along waterways and the cultivated land occupied a fairly narrow strip only a few kilometres in width on each bank.[22] On the periphery of the cultivated land was spasmodically utilised ground where beasts could graze at suitable times of the year and where fuel could be gathered. Beyond this was empty land which in many cases formed the neutral or buffer zone, between one political unit and the next; when no such buffer zone existed (as apparently in the case of Umma and Lagash) the sniping, and violation of peace treaties was incessant. It was this curious physical isolation which militated against the establishment of any real political hegemonies in the South and even in the time of nominal domination by one overlord seems to have made a considerable degree of autonomy possible among the subject cities. The frequent rebellions under even such a central-ised government as that of the early Agade kings[23] illustrate this well. One must not, however, over-emphasize the isolation of these city states; economics dictated that they were to some extent inter-reliant; not one of them was economically self-sufficient and the existence of trade routes over large areas must have neces-sitated a certain amount of inter-city co-operation in policing and maintaining these routes and in "servicing" the caravans. It seems probable that dynastic marriages played a considerable part in cementing friendly relationships between one city and another. The bead from Mari inscribed with the name of Mesannipadda of Ur was quite possibly from the dowry of a princess of Ur, in just such a dynastic marriage.[24] It is a platitude today to point out that the only native resources of Sumer were mud and reeds plus a little poor quality wood and stone. All other raw materials had to be imported and, the archaeological record shows that a wide range of utilitarian and luxury materials including gold, silver, copper, stone, wood, lapis lazuli, cornelian and obsidian were freely available by the beginning of the third millennium. The archaeological evidence is amplified by both factual economic texts and heroic stories in which trade plays an important, if sometimes implicit, part.[25]

It is hoped that the foregoing pages have provided a brief summary of the physical background against which the architec-ture of the third millennium can be analysed with the hope of attaining something more than a mere typology. The next task is to attempt to place the subject in its temporal setting.

One of the problems facing anyone who attempts a history of this early period is the problem of synthesizing the archaeological and the documentary evidence. The sequence in each field is clearly demonstrated by stratigraphy in one, and orthography in the other. It is when an attempt is made to place historically attested people and events in their archaeological context that conflict is likely to arise. Take, for example, the discussion which has raged now for nearly half a century on the relative chronology of the dynasties of Ur and Lagash and the position of Mesilim of Kish. Solutions proposed range from that of S.Pallis who sees Lugal-Zagisi of Uruk as the conqueror of the First Dynasty of Ur, to W.W.Hallo who makes the First Dynasty of Ur contemporary with both Gilgames and Mesilim.[26] In between comes H.J.Nissen who sees the foundation of the First Dynasty of Ur as subsequent to the raid on that town by Eannatum of Lagash.

If we take the archaeological evidence first, Henri Frankfort's division of the Early Dynastic period into three[27] is still the basic framework on which the chronology of the period hangs, although it is becoming increasingly clear that there is a strong case for a continuous development from the Jemdet Nasr phase into Early Dynastic I. This is demonstrated in the architectural continuity shown at several sites and also by the pottery.[28] Early Dynastic II has, on the other hand, expanded in importance and now looks to be the period at which characteristically Early Dynastic features and motifs first appear. The importance of Early Dynastic II as a period in its own right, and not merely as an awkward transition between Early Dynastic I and Early Dynastic III is well illustrated by the long series of Inanna temples at Nippur attributed to this phase. Interestingly, Early Dynastic II also seems to be the period to which social and political developments of considerable importance should be attributed. For example, it is "orthodox" to attribute the building of the city wall of Uruk by Gilgames to this period with the concomitant deductions that it was a period of increasing nationalism and of the expansion of the secular power of the ruler. However, the archaeological record is very incomplete and secular public building may yet be found in earlier periods as the result of further exploration. There is, for example, mention of a "public building" at T. Uquair in the Ubaid period and the "palace" at Jemdet Nasr.[29]

Early Dynastic III is a long period marked by stylistic developments in many fields (although by no striking innovations), perhaps most noticeably in statuary, glyptic art and metalwork, in all of which there is an increased dexterity and sophistication and a trend towards the naturalistic art which is such a feature of the succeeding Sargonid period. At Ur for example the period covers the Royal Cemetery and probably the overlying Grey Stratum in which were found the First Dynasty inscriptions. This rubbish stratum is no longer regarded as sealing off the Early Dynastic level of the Royal Cemetery.[30] It is convenient to divide this archaeologically amazingly productive period into two, IIIA and IIIB as Frankfort did. It is only in the Diyala and more recently at Nippur that it has been possible to establish a complete stratigraphic sequence covering the whole of the third millennium. At Lagash the evidence is hopelessly confused as it is at Adab. In the North both Gawra and Mari, the two outstanding sites, have lacunae in the sequence and the only general comment to be made is that the archaeological record, at least in the South, bears witness to great prosperity founded on an efficient exploitation of agricultural resources and a flourishing foreign trade whose contacts may well span the area between the Anatolian highlands and the west coast of India.

The Akkadian period is very poorly represented archaeologically and little can be said about it in terms of stratigraphy. The apparent abandonment of several important Early Dynastic sites at the beginning of the Agade period was one of the reasons for the assumption of inter-racial strife between Semites and Sumerians, but this abandonment should perhaps more realistically be explained in terms of erosion and a certain centralisation of the administration under Sargon. Recent surveys have also shown that there was a sharp drop in the sedentary population for reasons which we cannot at the moment explain. A further difficulty is encountered in that it is not easy to distinguish between Agade pottery and that of Isin Larsa and Ur III period.[31] The destruction wrought by the Guti and others at the end of the Sargonid period and the subsequent period of political uncertainty must have been responsible for the destruction and decay of many Akkadian public buildings, while the centralisation of authority probably cut down the number of such public buildings in provincial centres. An attempt to sub-divide the Akkadian period into three on the basis of the glyptic evidence[32] has been made but little is known of architectural plans or pottery forms. However, it is worth repeating that the available evidence shows that many Early Dynastic characteristics were incorporated in the material culture and no obvious attempt was made to suppress "Sumerian nationalism".[33]

Our second tool, the documentary evidence provides three major epigraphic milestones within the Early Dynastic period, the first an inscription of En-mebaragisi of Kish, the second of Mesilim, a lineal successor, and the third the group of inscriptions of Eannatum of Lagash. The relative dates of these inscriptions are not disputed, but the period of time separating each of them is.[34] En-mebaragisi was an older contemporary of Gilgames (En-mebaragisi is succeeded by Akka who is Gilgames's opponent in one of the epics). Gilgames is usually dated to the Early Dynastic II period. One reason for this dating is that in the Fara tablets, usually ascribed to Early Dynastic IIIA, Gilgames already has the divine determinative, that is to say, was already regarded as supra-human, and therefore must pre-date this period by several generations to have allowed this myth to develop. Mesilim is, orthographically speaking, more developed than En-mebaragisi and the one archaeological find securely dated to his lifetime is his inscribed mace head. Stylistically this piece seems to belong to the Early Dynastic II period.[35] It then follows that Gilgames must belong with En-mebaragisi to a period earlier than this, that is to say at latest to the early part of the Early Dynastic II.

The third epigraphic milestone comes from Lagash; Rowton describes Eannatum as being "the first ruler of Lagash whose inscriptions have an orthography virtually free of the archaic features which, gradually diminishing, are characteristic of the Early Dynastic epigraphic material".[36] On the other hand, archaeological evidence such as the use of plano-convex brick and the parallels between his Stele of the Vultures and the actual finds from the Royal Cemetery at Ur, place Eannatum firmly in the Early Dynastic III period. It seems likely that A-Anne-Padda of Ur was a near-contemporary, as his inscriptions are also free of archaisms, although the inscription of Kur-Lil found at Ubaid and thought to be contemporary, is not.[37] However, the possibility that this inscription dates to a period earlier than that of A-Anne-Padda and perhaps the founding of a smaller, older, shrine at Ubaid cannot be ruled out. Such a theory might go some way towards explaining the inequalities of the layout of the Ninkhursag temple at Ubaid and the somewhat archaic stylistic features of the statue of Kur-Lil himself.[38] The only obstacle to the synchronism of A-Anne-Padda and Eannatum is Eannatum's claim to have conquered Ur at a time when, if this synchronism is accepted, the First Dynasty of Ur was still powerful. It is, however, possible to skirt this difficulty by proposing that Eannatum's "conquest" of Ur was no more than a highly successful raiding party, perhaps in the reign of A-Anne-Padda's son Meskiag-Nannar when the power of the First Dynasty seems to have been already on the wane. The find of a clay cone inscribed with the name of Eannatum at Ur need not be ascribed to a military conquest either, a diplomatic exchange of gifts or even a dynastic marriage might explain it. Another archaeological reason for proposing the synchronism Eannatum/A-Anne-Padda is that the glyptic art of the period shows that stylistically Mes-Anne-Padda of Ur, A-Anne-Padda's predecessor, was not far removed from Urukagina of Lagash, Eannatum's fifth successor, and therefore should not be too far removed from him in time.[39]

Into this very loose framework of En-mebaragisi, and therefore Gilgames preceding Mesilim in Early Dynastic II or even late Early Dynastic I, Mesilim stylistically placed in Early Dynastic II, preceding Eannatum who is closely linked with A-Anne-Padda of the First Dynasty of Ur and Early Dynastic IIIB, must be fitted the Meskalam-Dug or Royal Cemetery Dynasty and Ur-Nanse of Lagash. The sophistication and elaboration of the art from the royal graves at Ur points to a considerable development from the time of Mesilim in Early Dynastic II, yet stratigraphically the Royal Cemetery precedes Dynasty I at Ur; there is no convincing evidence to suggest that some of the royal graves may date back to Early Dynastic II, and the Meskalam-Dug Dynasty may be placed in Early Dynastic IIIA, earlier than Dynasty I and later than Mesilim. Ur-Nanse of Lagash is stylistically close to the Meskalam-Dug Dynasty and yet cannot be much more than two generations away from A-Anne-Padda whose inscriptions, as we have said, link him orthographically with Eannatum, Ur-Nanse's second successor.

Archaeologically a lot hinges on the deposition of the grey rubbish stratum S.I.S. 1/2 which lies above the Royal Cemetery at Ur. Rubbish would surely not have been deposited on a royal graveyard in the period immediately succeeding that Dynasty; the rubbish contained First Dynasty inscriptions. These could have come from looted graves below the grey stratum or could be contemporary with it. If the former is the case, then S.I.S. 1/2 was probably not deposited until after the end of the First Dynasty; if the second is the case then S.I.S. 1/2 was probably deposited during Dynasty I and might be the result of a tidying-up operation after destruction in the city caused by, say, the raid by Eannatum; much of the rubbish is said to be brick rubble. This would allow for a respectable passage of time between the digging of the last of the pre-dynastic royal graves and the dumping of the rubbish in the graveyard. In the event of the sack of the city, much of the rubble would have to be carted out to the periphery before rebuilding could get under way, and inscribed fragments could well be included in it. The second proposition is perhaps the more attractive and may mean that the First Dynasty cemetery is still to be found!

One problem which this scheme does not resolve is the relative dating of En-shakus-Anna, son of Elulu, penultimate ruler of the First Dynasty of Ur and Lugal-kinisi-dudu (and his son Lugal-kisalsi) with whom Entemena of Lagash made a treaty and who claimed kingship of Uruk, Ur, Umma and Kish.[40] En-shakus-Anna appears to have been given the rulership of Uruk by his father Elulu, while his brother Balulu ruled Ur, possibly as a vassal, for En-shakus-Anna claimed the prestige title of En Kengi, En Kalama. His son Lugal-Kinisi-Dudu ruled both Ur and Uruk and was sufficiently powerful to conclude a treaty with the apparently then ageing Entemena of Lagash and hand on his kingdom to his son Lugal-Kisalsi who, in his turn, was supplanted by Lugal-Zagisi the conqueror of Urukagina of Lagash. This scheme avoids having to compress the first and second Ur Dynasties as H.J.Nissen has done, by making Mes-Anne-Padda closer to Ur-Nanse rather than a later contemporary of Eannatum. The compression would not seem to allow sufficient time for the great quantity of archaeological remains dated to Early Dynastic IIIA and B at both Ur and Lagash. This scheme would mean a fairly short reign for Balulu of Ur who may have been a brother of En-shakus-Anna, if not his uncle. Another uneasy problem is raised by the Tummal inscription[41] but archaeologically and orthographically, for reasons quoted above, it is impossible for Mes-Anne-Padda and Gilgames to be contemporary, unless of course the tradition which links Gilgames with En-mebaragisi can be shown to be a corrupt one.

To sum up, En-mebaragisi and Gilgames on both orthographic and archaeological grounds may be placed in Early Dynastic I/II; Mesilim belongs to Early Dynastic II, the Fara tablets and the Meskalam-Dug Dynasty to Early Dynastic IIIA, and the First Dynasty of Ur and the Lagashite Dynasty from Eannatum to Urukagina to Early Dynastic IIIB. Ur-Nanse hovers on the divide between Early Dynastic IIIA and IIIB, stylistically closer to IIIA. The Sargonid period, comparatively speaking at least, is lucid; such were the advantages of centralised authority. One dynasty ruled without serious interruption for a length of time which by archaeological standards can be accurately defined even if the relative dating of events within the period is not so well understood.[42]

Finally, an attempt must be made to express the relative chronology expressed above in absolute terms. It should be stressed that at this distance in time the relative sequence of events is of greater importance than their absolute dates. These, even at best, with plentiful documentation and the refinement of modern scientific methods, can never be more than approximations, subject in some cases to deviations of more than a century in either direction. If we first look at the later documentary evidence we are able to deduce an average date of c.2300 B.C. for the accession of Sargon, and c.2150 for the end of the Akkad Dynasty, depending on which date is accepted for the accession of Hammurabi of Babylon, that vital and much disputed peg on which hangs so much of the chronology of the Middle East.[43] Working backwards from here, H.J.Nissen[44] allows 160 years between Sargon and Ur-Nanse, with a further 50 years back to the Fara tablets, usually regarded as being on the divide between Early Dynastic II and Early Dynastic IIIA. The fifty years allowed between the Fara tablets and Ur-Nanse would in the scheme proposed here be filled by the royal graves at Ur for which 50 years seems a minimal time span and a hundred more convincing. Let us then suppose that Early Dynastic III began about 2550 B.C. The documentary evidence cannot be of much help beyond this point although Nissen would allow another fifty years between the Fara tablets and Gilgames, placing Gilgames about 2600. Once again this seems too little both on archaeological grounds and because of the fact, mentioned above, that in the Fara tablets Gilgames's name is written with the divine determinative, indicating that he was already by that time a legend.

We are now obliged to turn to other methods of absolute dating for the period before that of Gilgames, i.e. c.2650 B.C., and we are immediately faced with the contradictions between the dates deduced from the internal evidence and those provided by C^{14} determination, which have been found to be about 450 years younger than expected in some cases; for example, the average C^{14} date for the Early Dynastic I levels at Nippur is given as c.2250 B.C..[45] However, work by Hans Suess on the calibration of the time scale obtained by C^{14} determination with that obtained by dendrochronology has considerably altered the picture as Braidwood has shown. The average Nippur date for Early Dynastic I now reads as c.2900 B.C. which fits much better into our scheme. If a rough and ready attempt is made to convert other C^{14} dates the results are also promising. Of three recently published dates from Jemdat Nasr, one falls within the expected time range and gives a corrected date of 2859±140: the other two dates appear to be too young and a fourth seems to be contaminated.[46] The controversial dates obtained from skeletons from the royal graves give a converted date of c.2,500, which is only slightly lower than one would expect. It must be remembered that statistically speaking, there is only two chances out of three that the date produced falls within the tolerance expressed.

Our evidence in the North is even more fragmentary. With the exception of Mari, king lists are not known for the North and we are thrown back on the archaeological record alone for dating material. Once more the broad outline of the period is reasonably clear as some comparisons can be made between artefacts and buildings in the two areas. The C^{14} dates from the Jazirah mostly relate to the earlier periods and although, as in the South, the uncorrected dates are later than we would expect, Joan Oates has shown that on the whole the dates for the Samarra/Halaf material are internally consistent and suggest a date of c.5,000 B.C. for the

late Ubaid.[47] In the third millennium we have only a date from
T. eth Thalathat in a level associated with Ninevite V pottery, that
is to say E.D.I/Jemdat Nasr in Southern terms, which yields a
roughly corrected date of c.2,700 B.C. This fits in reasonably well
with the evidence we have quoted from the South.[48]

To sum up, the relative dating is reasonably convincing and
what is badly needed to enable us to express this relative sequence
in absolute terms is firstly, a stratified sequence of C^{14} dates
covering the whole of the third millennium, and more difficult to
achieve a measure of agreement on the correction necessary and
on the relationship between C^{14} years and calendar years. It is to
be hoped that excavations at Nippur and T. Taya may produce the
former. Until new evidence becomes available all that we can say is
that there is nothing in the corrected C^{14} dates which makes the
conventional dates of c.2,800–2,200 B.C. for the Early Dynastic
and Agade periods untenable. There is a possibility that these dates
may have to be expanded a little in either direction.

NOTES

[1] R.J.Braidwood and B.Howe, *Prehistoric Investigations in Iraqi Kurdistan*,
and more recently, Hole, Flannery and Neely, *The prehistory and human
ecology of Deh Luran*.

[2] For a good summary, cf. A.J.Jawad, *The advent of the era of townships
in North Mesopotamia*, pp. 8–16; A.L.Oppenheim, *Ancient Mesopotamia*, pp. 35–48; R.McC.Adams,*The land behind Baghdad*; D.Oates,
Studies in the ancient history of N. Iraq; M.A.Beek, *Atlas of Mesopotamia*; C.E.Larsen, 'The Mesopotamian Delta Region', *J.A.O.S.* 95.1,
pp. 43–58; G.M.Lees and N.R.Falcon, 'Geographical history of the
Mesopotamian plains', *Geog. J.*, 118, p. 24. The following section is
based on the above unless specific references are given. For climatic
evidence, cf. K.W.Butzer, *C.A.H. Prolegomena*, Chap. II, and R.Raikes,
Water, Weather and Prehistory.

[3] T.Jacobsen and R.McC.Adams,'Salt and Silt and ancient Mesopotamian
Agriculture', in *Science* 128, p.1251; S.D.Walters, *Waters of Larsa*; On
deforestation, Braidwood *et al*, *op. cit.*, p. 170–173.

[4] R.McC.Adams and H.Nissen,*The Uruk countryside*, pp. 6–7.

[5] Adams and Nissen, *op. cit.*, *passim* and McG.Gibson, *The City and area
of Kish*.

[6] H.E.W.Crawford, 'Stimuli towards urbanisation in S. Mesopotamia', in *Man, Settlement and Urbanism*, eds. P.Ucko, R.Tringham and G.W. Dimbleby, p. 761.

[7] G.Le Strange, *Lands of the Eastern Caliphate*, Chap. I and Map I.

[8] For a general discussion, A.L.Oppenheim, *Ancient Mesopotamia*, p. 49, and I.J.Gelb, 'Sumerians and Akkadians in their ethno-linguistic relationship', in *Genava* 8, 1960, p. 247.

[9] For a recent summary, M.E.L.Mallowan in *C.A.H.* I, Chap. VIII, pt. i, and T.B.Jones, *The Sumerian Problem*: A very useful summing up of the pros and cons of the argument.

[10] G.Bibby, *Looking for Dilmun*.

[11] For a summary of the finds from T.Chuera, M.E.L.Mallowan in *Iraq* XXVIII, p. 89. For a discussion of the Sumerian style statuary, A.Moortgat, *Art of Ancient Mesopotamia*, p. 36, pls. 70, 71, and the interim reports.

[12] The homogeneity of culture at Mari is well illustrated both by the long series of temples and by the superimposed palaces, cf. A.Parrot, *Le Temple d'Ishtar*, and *Reports on the Palace in Syria* XLII and XLIV.

[13] A.Parrot, *M.A.M.* III, p. 307.

[14] T.B.Jones, *op. cit.*, p. 104.

[15] A.Moortgat, *op. cit.*, p. 45.

[16] For a general study of the Semites, S.Moscati, *The Semites in Ancient History*, especially Chaps. I, II.

[17] A.Moortgat, *op. cit.*, p. 35 for Semitic inscriptions and T.Jacobsen, *The Sumerian Kinglist*.

[18] D.Wilson, *The Anglo-Saxons*, Intro. and Chap. 5.

[19] J.van Dijk, *Les contacts ethniques dans la Mésopotamie - - -*, especially p. 203 on Syncretism. Papers read at a symposium on cultural contacts at Åbo 1966, ed. by S.S.Hartmann. For the contrary view, T.Jacobsen, 'The assumed conflict between Sumerians and Semites in early Mesopotamian history', *J.A.O.S.* 59, 1939, pp. 485–495.

[20] H.J.Nissen, *Zur Datierung des Königsfriedhofes von Ur*. Table 6, p. 75 shows the continuity of pottery types between E.D.III/Agade.

[21] For the movement of Bedu out of cities, cf. W.Caskel as quoted by Moscati, *op. cit.*, p. 34. Also Adams and Nissen, *op. cit.*, p. 37.

[22] H.T.Wright, 'Rural production in Mesopotamia'. *Anth. papers no. 38*, Museum of Anth., University of Michigan.

[23] E.Sollberger and J.R.Kupper, *Inscriptions Royales Sumériennes et Akkadiennes*, pp. 97–112.

[24] A.Parrot, 'Le trésor d'Ur'. *M.A.M*, IV, p. 53. Note also the controversy

about the reading of the inscription; E.Sollberger, *R.A.* 63, 1969, pp. 169–170, and G.Dossin, *R.A.* 64, 1970, pp. 163–168.

25 C.C.Lamberg-Karlovsky, 'Trade mechanisms in Indus/Mesopotamian interrelations', in *J.A.O.S.* 92.2, p. 222.

26 S.Pallis, *The Shubad-ad culture*; W.W.Hallo and W.K.Simpson, *The Ancient Near East*, pp. 42–46 and fig. 8. For another useful summary and assessment, cf. M.B.Rowton in *C.A.H.* Vol. I, Chap. VI.

27 H.Frankfort, *O.I.C.* 20, p. 35.

28 M.E.L.Mallowan, *C.A.H.*, Vol. I, pt. 2, Chap. XVI, pp. 238–240; E.Porada in *Chronologies in old world archaeology*, ed. Ehrich, p. 160.

29 T.Uquair, S.Lloyd in *J.N.E.S.* II, No. 2, p. 149 and pl. VIb; Jemdet Nasr palace, *Der Alte Orient* XXVI 1927, Fig. 12.

30 H.E.W.Crawford, *Unpublished doctoral thesis* University of London, 1962; cf. also R.Maxwell-Hyslop, *Western Asiatic Jewellery*, p. 2.

31 Adams and Nissen, *op. cit.*, p. 37.

32 R.M.Boehmer, *Die Entwicklung der Glyptik während der Akkad zeit.*

33 For instance, the typical combat scene of E.D.II/III remains a favourite motif in the Akkadian period.

34 For a discussion of the orthography, D.O.Edzard, 'Enmebaragesi von Kish', in *Z.f.A.* 53, p. 9ff.

35 A stele of uncertain provenance, illustrated by Moortgat in *The Art of ancient Mesopotamia* pls. 31–34 belongs to the same period. The bunched up kilts worn by some of the men portrayed on the stele are a characteristic of the glyptic of E.D.II.

36 M.B.Rowton, *C.A.H.*, Vol. I, pt. i, Chap. VI, p. 222.

37 Rowton, *op. cit.*, p. 222. Note that C.J.Gadd in H.R.Hall's, *Al Ubaid*, p. 133, holds that "the whole of the inscribed material from Ubaid appears to be homogenenous in time."

38 For instance, his angular elbows and uncomprising solidity. For the possibility that the statue belonged to an earlier shrine, cf. H.J.Nissen, *op. cit.*, p. 136.

39 A.Moortgat, *op. cit.*, p. 41.

40 For royal inscriptions, cf. Sollberger and Kupper, *op. cit.*, and for a general summary, Rowton, *op. cit.*, esp. p. 222–223 and table on p. 237; also A.Goetze, 'Early Kings of Kish', *J.C.S.* 15, p. 105.

41 For the Tunmal inscription, E.Sollberger in *J.C.S.* XVI, p. 40 and S.N.Kramer in *Gilgames et sa legende*', ed. P.Garelli, p. 59.

42 For the chronology of the Agade period, cf. Rowton, *op. cit.*, p. 219. An example of the comparatively minor revolts which occurred within the period is given in the hymn *The exultation of Inanna*, ed. W.W.Hallo and

Van Dijk, when Ur seems to have been temporarily "liberated" from Sargonid rule.

[43] Rowton, *op. cit. passim.*

[44] Nissen, *op. cit.*, p. 142.

[45] R.Braidwood in *Sumer* XXIII, 1967, p. 39. 'Radioactive Carbon Age Determination. For the chart correllating the dates obtained by C^{14} and dendrochronology, see most recently, R.Derricourt in *J.N.E.S.* 30, No. 4, p. 271, Fig. 1. Date from T. eth Thalathat, *Radiocarbon* II, No. 2, p. 513. Date from Royal Graves at Ur, *Radiocarbon* 3, p. 43.

[46] These samples were apparently obtained during surface surveys and there is a high possibility of contamination, *Radiocarbon* 14.i, p. 147.

[47] J.Oates, 'A radiocarbon date from Choga Mami', *Iraq* XXXIV.i, p. 49.

[48] *Radiocarbon* II,2, p. 513.

CHAPTER II

Architecture in the South

The architectural remains of a culture are potentially one of the richest sources of information available to the archaeologist. Even when the excavations which uncovered the buildings were carried out in the pioneer days of exploration and lack the finesse which can be achieved today, the architectural evidence often survives more or less intact and provides us with a valuable index of technological achievement and change, social organisation and religious doctrine, as well as many impressive monuments. Unfortunately the scale of operations in the Near East has militated against the collection of "micro-evidence" which would allow us to attempt the exhaustive analysis of artefact distribution and room utilization which is now being attempted in other fields with interesting results. Nor can we attempt an analysis of the positioning of buildings within a settlement, another potentially fruitful line of approach.[1] Our material is limited, unbalanced and unrepresentative. The early excavators, blatantly looking for loot, concentrated their energies on monumental buildings in large settlements of obvious importance and often physical prominence. Our evidence is therefore heavily overweighted with "palaces" and "temples", some of which were extensively damaged by tunnelling and gouging, both by the excavators and by the treasure-seeking local inhabitants. We have little evidence for domestic architecture, town planning or industrial activities. The indifference of the early excavators to these fields may mean that much of the evidence is still waiting undisturbed for a more scientifically-minded modern approach. However, in the case of industrial activities, it may be that there is little evidence available; two of the key industries in the third millennium for export seem to have been weaving and tanning of which certainly the former need leave little in the way of archaeological remains. A charming model of a weaving shop from the tomb of Meket-Re at Thebes illustrates the weaving techniques used in Egypt c.2000 B.C.;[2] the archaeological evidence for such a workshop would appear likely to be four small post holes in the floor and six peg holes in the walls, if these were preserved to sufficient height. A seal impression from Susa shows the same techniques in use in the 3rd millennium. Using modern ethnographical comparisons it also seems likely that there was a thriving cottage industry in many urban and rural settlements, where the family income was supplemented by weaving or spinning of wool, flax and reeds.[3] Here again the archaeological evidence would be minimal and indeed we have little knowledge of small rural communities in the third millennium at all; even if field survey has located such settlements they have seldom been excavated.[4] As mentioned earlier, the preference until recently has been for monumental architecture.

By the third millennium the builder had mastered the basic mechanics of building in mud-brick. He could build arches, vaults and domes; he constructed sophisticated drainage systems both to deal with sewage and to distribute fresh water. He built magnificent fortifications and impressive ceremonial entrances. The ubiquitous mud-brick was made into pillars and stairs; when baked it was practically weatherproof and when coated with bitumen waterproof. Stone was still used only sparingly and wood appears to have been used mainly for roof beams. Poorer homes seem to have been made of wattle and daub and perhaps also of reed mats; even in the north where stone was more freely available mud-brick was the predominant building material. The Early Dynastic period is characterised in the south by the use of the plano-convex brick which has long been regarded as a type fossil for the period. It is however becoming increasingly clear that this unwieldy brick was not in fact universally introduced at the beginning of Early Dynastic I and that it continued in use into the Agade period.[5] On its own it can no longer be regarded as conclusive proof of Early Dynastic date even when laid in the characteristic herring-bone pattern which perhaps derives from the patterns woven into reed mats. An example of this type of brickwork dated to the Agade period has recently been found near Kish at Umm-el-jir.[6] The fact that any structure made of plano-convex brick has in the past automatically been attributed to the Early Dynastic period may go some way towards explaining the paucity of excavated material from the early part of the Agade period when, as we have just shown, the plano-convex brick was actually still in use. For instance it seems possible that at Uruk Ziggurat I[1] [7] should be dated to the Agade period. The bricks used are slightly plano-convex, hence its present attribution to the Early Dynastic period, but this period already covers a considerable amount of material from Level II and Levels I[2-7]. At present there are no remains at Uruk dated to the Agade period.

In this chapter the names given to buildings by the excavators have been adhered to even when modern evidence suggests that they may be misnomers. The term "palace" is one which has been considerably overworked in the past and which today should perhaps be replaced with a less emotive description such as administrative centre, barracks, or even factory. Many of the large buildings probably in fact combined several of these functions along with those of schools, law courts and store houses.

An attempt will first be made to describe temple architecture in the third millennium, grouping this evidence loosely into six categories:

A. Classic tripartite plans
B. Single room shrines.
C. Bipartite shrines.
D. House plan temples.
E. Temple ovals.
F. Miscellaneous.

Group A is represented by the earliest phases of the Sin temple at Khafaje. From Level I–V, Jemdet Nasr in date, the Sin temple shows the classic features of the tripartite temple with an adjoining court service area as well. It is interesting to notice how this service area expands and by the beginning of Early Dynastic I is incorporated firmly in the temple area by means of an enclosure wall entered up a flight of steps. In fact Sin VI seems to represent an intermediate stage in the apparent development from tripartite plans to plans of our Group D, the House Plan temples.[8] In Sin IV the temple, though not the court, is placed on a platform for the first time, a practical arrangement whose theological implications have perhaps been overestimated.

The single room shrines of Group B with two exceptions, appear to belong to the early part of the period. The earliest example seems to come from the chapel at T. Uquair, but no details are given in an excavation report. The chapel is associated with Jemdet Nasr pottery. The next example from Sumer proper comes from the Inanna Temple at Nippur where in Levels VII–VIII, dated by the excavators to Early Dynastic II, the more southerly of the two shrines is a simple single room shrine with an entrance in the west wall to give a bent axis approach; by contrast the Uquair example has a direct axis approach.[9] The other examples come from the Diyala and show considerable modification as the plan expands; at Khafaje both the Small Temple and the Nintu Temple, founded at the beginning of the Early Dynastic period, began as single rooms with a bent axis approach from the North-east. The Nintu temple with its handsome buttressing is the more sophisticated and its later development to include two courtyards and two further shrines is also more elaborate. The Small Temple merely develops an increasingly large courtyard or service area and both seem to have been deserted by Early Dynastic IIIa. A third example from Khafaje is the Small Single Shrine founded in Early Dynastic IIIb; this has the buttressing of the Nintu temple with a recessed entrance on the long north wall[10] to give a bent axis approach. The Single Shrine Abu Temple at T. Asmar founded in Early Dynastic III resembles the earliest Nintu temple with buttressing on the corners and external face of the walls and an entrance on the north wall at right angles to the altar. Here again the plan is significantly modified in later Agade levels and the shrine is in fact divided into two, the entrance to the ante-chamber remaining unaltered but an entrance was built from the antechamber into the cella, opposite the altar, giving a direct axis approach.[11] It becomes in effect a member of our Group C, the bipartite temples. There is no evidence at the moment to support an assertation that Group C generally developed from Group B.

There are five bipartite temples in Group C, one from T. Asmar, two from Nippur and two from Tello. At T. Asmar the earliest Abu shrine of "Protoliterate" date is basically a member of this group in spite of its rather tortured plan, dictated presumably by the surrounding buildings. From Nippur we have the older Inanna shrine of Levels IX—XI which consists of a broad anteroom and cella with direct axis approach. It is interesting to note that the excavators state that the cella was unroofed. There is also a small asymmetrically placed service room behind the altar. The more northerly of the shrines in the succeeding Early Dynastic II levels is also bipartite, and, unusually, has two entrances, one on the direct axis, and one on the side wall.[12] Two examples come from Tello; of the Maison des Fruits, little can constructively be said; the lower building known as the Construction Inferieure is bipartite and although there is no communication between the two halves they may be a cella and antechamber, perhaps the mirror image of a temple now vanished, which stood above it. Examples of such mirror-image temples are known from the Enlil Temple at Nippur and from El Hibba. Above this is the shrine of Ur-Nanshe the two halves of which are actually separated by a passage although associated by an encircling outer wall. The smaller of the two rooms has the shape of an E without the middle stroke. The association of this building with Ur-Nanshe dates it to Early Dynastic IIIa.[13]

We have only two examples of the House Plan temples of Group D, a type which reoccurs in the North. The finest example is the square temple from T. Asmar which in its essentials is the idealised ordinary house plan, with its central court originally with rooms on three sides only, the range on the fourth side seems to have been added later as it is not wholly symmetrical.[14] This was surely an entirely appropriate plan for a temple where the god lived, was fed and clothed as well as worshipped. The drawing board ideal of the Square Temple is not reflected in the later Sin temple layout at Khafaje, another House Plan temple, where the classic pattern seems to have been fairly drastically altered. The Early Dynastic I temple of Sin VI seems to mark a transition from the earlier Tripartite Plan to the House Plan temples which are not found before the Early Dynastic period. Basically we still have a courtyard round which lie shrines, offices and living quarters.[15] Similar modifications of the classic house plan are very noticeable in a study of the houses of the town, where the exigencies of space can considerably alter the theoretical plan. The Sin temple in its final stages has three parallel shrines on the west side of the court[16] which seems to indicate not only an increase in prosperity, but also an elaboration of ritual.

It is suggested that different temple plans were appropriate to different gods and that this might explain the lack of standardisation in the plans of the third millennium temples, which have come down to us. In particular a group of Oval temple enclosures have been identified and are thought to be a form dedicated to female deities. These form our Group E and examples are known to us from Khafaje, Ubaid, El Hibba and Bahrein. The date of the last is somewhat uncertain, but falls within the second half of the third millennium. The temples at Ubaid and El Hibba are dedicated to Ninkhursag and Inanna respectively. In each case the enclave consists of single or double enclosure walls within which, at Khafaje[17] the most complete of the plans, lies a central courtyard which must originally have housed a shrine probably on a platform or ziggurat now completely destroyed; offering places; stores; workrooms and service rooms, all lie within the courtyard. The complex of rooms known as House D at Khafaje lies between the inner and the outer encircling walls. Its plan conforms to that of the standard private house and the excavators suggested it as a *Giparu*, the official dwelling of the *En* priest. At Ubaid only the ornamentation of the facade of the temple was recovered, standing on its platform in the double oval enclosure. As work has only just begun at El Hibba it is not yet clear whether the rooms already excavated are indeed part of a temple or if they are service rooms round the edge of the enclosure with a possible shrine in the centre of the court. The elaboration observed in the foundation of these rooms does strongly suggest that they are part of a temple and no trace has yet been found of a central platform. The temple at Bahrein does not strictly concern us and its plan shows some atypical features such as a deep cistern or well.[18]

Finally we come to Group F, to the Archaic Temple at T. Asmar and the Shara Temple at T. Agrab, neither of which will fit into any of our categories. There is also a group of temples known to us only from inscriptions, such as the famous Tummal at Nippur[19] and one or two, like the temple at Adab,[20] where early excavators failed to recover the plan or where as in the Enlil

Temple at Nippur the early plan was practically destroyed by later rebuilding.[21] It is curious that no temples of this period have been found at Kish which boasted two ziggurats. It has been suggested that the plano-convex brick debris mentioned as lying below Monument Z, in the shadow of the larger ziggurat, might well represent the remains of such a temple.[22] Ur is also poorly provided with third millennium temples especially if we regard the two "kitchen" temples at the foot of the ziggurat as being service rooms or possibly residential quarters for the priests on duty. Penelope Weadock has suggested that the Ur III *Giparu* was probably preceded by an earlier one of Sargonid or Early Dynastic date.[23] To return to the Archaic Temple at T. Asmar, the excavated portion is only a segment of a larger unit and may perhaps be paralleled most nearly by the "Enceinte Sacrée" in the palace at Mari, that is to say it was part of a larger, probably multi-purpose unit. The same is true of the Shara Temple at T. Agrab[24] and it seems possible that the Early Dynastic II Inanna shrines at Nippur may also be part of a larger, possibly secular complex. The internal arrangement of the main Shara shrine has features in common with the Early Dynastic III Sin temple at Khafaje where one of the shrines also has a double row of offering tables or prieux-dieu.

If we look now at the evidence for the Agade period only one of the temples known from the Early Dynastic period can definitely be said to have survived. The Abu Single Shrine at T. Asmar[25] survived, where its more impressive contemporaries did not, and appears to follow the plan of its predecessors, a rectangular, buttressed shrine and antechamber with adjacent service area. It is possible that the Temple Oval at Khafaje also survived into the early Agade period. Apart from this the sum of our information is provided by a few fragmentary walls below the Enlil Temple at Nippur, where the Inanna temple provides no architectural evidence at all, the only find being a macehead inscribed with the name of Naram-Sin. It is interesting to remember that in later tradition Naram-Sin is accused of having sacked Nippur. At Adab[27] Banks reports the finding of Sargonid brick and fragments of gold with the name of Naram-Sin on them, but no architectural remains. This meagre paragraph merely serves to underline the paucity of evidence from the Agade period.

Closely associated with temples in the Early Dynastic and Agade periods, were the ziggurats. There can now be little doubt that some sort of staged tower does go back to the Early Dynastic period, although there is no evidence for an earlier occurrence.[28] Langdon at Kish claimed to have found a ziggurat Z.1, which had four receding stages; the structure is built of plano-convex brick, but of the four stages there is no positive proof. A second tower, Z.2, was also found at Kish and appears to be slightly later in date as it actually overlies the ruins of a plano-convex brick building.[29] C.S.Fisher at Nippur also describes a ziggurat of "several receding stages" though once again there appears to be no basis of fact for this claim. Hilprecht, speaking more realistically of the same edifice, states that the smooth plastered face of a pre-Sargonid ziggurat was uncovered in a couple of places.[30] At Adab there was in Banks' words, "A staged temple tower of plano-convex brick laid in lime and ornamented with small deep[31] sockets", perhaps analagous to the "weeper" holes in some of the early temple platforms. From the insufficient plan given the tower seems to be more or less square, the east corner being extended by an area measuring approximately 2 x 8 m., possibly the remains of a ramp or stairs. The presence of a double enclosure wall is also mentioned. At Tello there is no ziggurat, but fragmentary remains of the so-called Massif of Entemena could be the last vestiges of one.[32] It is made of well-laid baked brick bonded with bitumen. At Ur the Early Dynastic ziggurat is completely engulfed by that of Ur-Nammu, but its existence can be safely deduced from the remains of the period in the surrounding courtyard area.[33] At Uruk the excavators claim that their structure is a high terrace, rather than a true ziggurat, but again the evidence to settle the question will probably never be forthcoming. It is a particularly interesting structure as it appears to be L-shaped in Level II, a shape found in the earlier Jamdet Nasr platform of Level IIIa and which continues into I[6]. The ziggurat area at Uruk is of special interest as it gives us some conception of the complexity of the organisation surrounding the administration of a major temple. It is difficult to know whether some of the neighbouring buildings should be classed as religious or not; certainly in the Jemdet Nasr period they included a metal-working compound[34] as well as the more conventional courtyards and offerings places, each unit apparently being separated from the next by roads each with its own gateway out of the perimeter wall.

Once again the evidence for the Agade period is meagre in the extreme; the only firm evidence for an Akkadian ziggurat comes from Nippur where Naram-Sin undertook extensive building operations in the ziggurat area. A platform of bricks stamped with his name underlies one corner of the present ziggurat and drains and pavements in the courtyard bear further witness to his activities.[35] As mentioned before this seems curiously at variance with later tradition that Naram-Sin destroyed Nippur thus bringing on himself the "Curse of Akkad".[36] Of the other ziggurats the ones at Kish appear to have fallen into disrepair, though Akkadian graves testify that the area was still in use as a cemetery. At Adab Banks found Sargonid bricks in the ziggurat mound and it seems legitimate to deduce the continued existence of a ziggurat here.[37] There is no evidence from Tello, and finally as mentioned before there is the possibility that at Uruk Eanna I[1] is in fact Early Agade in date. This concludes the survey of the religious buildings and we must now turn to the major secular buildings.

Excavations have produced examples of several buildings of sufficient complexity and elaboration to be called "Palaces" by their discoverers. From the admittedly incomplete plans of these buildings it seems that they have certain features in common. They are sub-divided into smaller units by means of passages. These smaller units are more or less self-contained, bonded together by a heavy, often fortified perimeter wall with a passage on the inside of it. This passage seems to have served several different purposes, it was defensively sound and must have provided a measure of insulation against noise and heat, as well as being the means of internal communication. Some of the individual units within these large complexes appear to have had specialist functions while others appear to be residential. Perhaps it is possible that these last reflect the custom which is well known from the texts of giving a ruler's wife and one at least of his sons, separate households of their own.[38] It has always been assumed that these were separate buildings, but possibly they were self-contained units within one perimeter wall. The earliest example and the least easy to elucidate is the so-called palace at Jemdet Nasr. It is associated with typical Jemdet-Nasr small finds and must in part at least date to this period. It has an outer zingel or enclosure wall with intramural rooms and seems to be divided internally into several distinct areas, one of which has a flight of stairs. It is perhaps possible that all the buildings shown on the plan are not contemporaneous, but on the other hand no small finds of a later date are reported from within the building. Possibly the "thick wide platform" in the centre of the building is later in date, it is certainly without parallel at the other "palaces". Finally it is possibly significant that most of these "palaces" seem to have been abandoned at the end of the Early Dynastic period. If they were primarily administrative and governmental buildings the Sargonid kings with their policy of centralisation would very likely transfer the seat of government in an attempt to curb the independence of these traditionally autonomous Early Dynastic centres such as Kish.

Kish has produced two such public buildings of which the better preserved is known as Palace A.[39] It has the only example of a monumental entrance in this class of building with a buttressed, recessed, doorway approached by a flight of steps. Two of the units within the original building are still extant and there must originally have been at least two more. One of the existing units, the one lying North-west of the entrance, is plainly residential while the second unit, South-west of the entrance, is unusual in that it was clearly added later as it destroys the symmetry of the entrance; it was perhaps designed as a reception and audience quarter; the pillared court and long reception room, 43 and 45, would fulfil these functions admirably. There is a lack of ordinary amenities such as kitchens which argues against it being residential. Possibly more living quarters lay in the unexcavated area to the south. The Plano-Convex Brick[40] building recently published by Moorey is another impressive building of which we have only a portion; this appears to be a service area with fairly extensive drainage arrangements and the remains of three structures which Moorey interprets as kilns or ovens. North of the courtyard lie the remains of a possible wine-press and North-west of this again lies what may well have been the residential section surrounded as usual by a passage, rooms XVII, XX and XXIII. The external wall is regularly buttressed and a functional rather than ceremonial entrance lay on the North side of the complex.

At Eridu we have a section of another large building[41] within which lay at least three units of which only one has been fully excavated. This section is distinguished by the number of small cell-like rooms nos. 14, 18, 20, 24, 26 and 27 and again rooms 41, 42 and 43. These would appear to be magazines for storage. Of the rest of the building we can say little except that there appears once again to be a passage encircling the northern half of the building. A door lies on the east wall, which is the only one with buttresses, but once again is obviously utilitarian, a tradesman's entrance.

A much robbed example of a building in a similar style comes from T.Wilayah,[42] where the lack of any distinguishing features has led the excavators to regard it as a residential area. New excavations at Uruk are uncovering a building named by the excavators the Stämpflehmgebaude[43] which lies north-west of the ziggurat. It appears to date back to the Jemdet Nasr period and to continue in use until the Agade period. From the description it seems to have certain features in common with the "Palaces" described above. There is said to be a passage no. 128 which may run round a considerable part of the building. The rooms are grouped in units round courtyards and there is a series of small, long, narrow rooms, possibly for storage. Further information about this building will be most interesting. From Ur we have on the E.H. site a heavily buttressed wall,[44] which may have belonged to a public building and is the only trace of such a building at Ur in this period. Finally we have a plano-convex building at T. Asmar,[45] adjacent to the Abu temple and lying below the Northern "Palace". Delougaz has argued cogently that this building was a small industrial centre. The new evidence from Uruk of metal working and potting adjacent to the ziggurat area makes the possibility even more attractive.

In the Agade period only two of these buildings seem to continue in use, the "palace" at Wilayah continued to be used although several of the rooms were blocked off, a further indication perhaps of the centralising of authority or of poverty. The excavators also claim that the Stampflehmgebaude at Uruk continued in use. At Kish the A palace was used as a graveyard in the Agade period and one intrusive grave in the P.C.B. building indicates that it too fell into disrepair at the end of Early Dynastic III. S.Lloyd has suggested that the fragmentary Monument Z at Kish may be Akkadian, but Moorey prefers to regard it as Ur III. Two new buildings appear, firstly the so-called Northern Palace at T. Asmar, lying above the earlier L-shaped plano-convex building. It is remarkable chiefly for the large numbers of "toilets" and an elaborate system of drains linked with a main sewer in the road. It does not have any of the monumental features associated with the other "Palaces" of Mesopotamia and the explanation that it is a work area possibly devoted to tanning, and perhaps metal-working, is a convincing one. Secondly, there is a brief description of a large rectangular building of Akkadian date at Khafaje. The north-eastern section of this building is clearly a residential unit, which seems to have had extra units tacked onto it, including two large courtyards and what may have been a chapel or possibly some sort of meeting hall. A parallel for the juxtaposition of public rooms and living quarters comes from Tepe Gawra. The brief list of small finds indicates that the inhabitants were relatively well-to-do and suggests the presence of an upper income bracket family, perhaps that of a town official.[46] Finally de Sarzac reported the discovery of an "enclosure" apparently of Sargonid date,[47] in which were found Agade tablets in bulk, on the Tell des Tablettes at Tello; these may well be the archives attached to a temple or palace.

We have now established the presence of large buildings indicative of some central authority, though it is not easy to tell whether it is a secular or a religious one, or indeed how valid this distinction is in the Early Dynastic period. Nor it is easy to distinguish the exact functions of these buildings, again possibly because the boundaries between politics, economics and religious affairs did not exist in the absolute way to which we are now accustomed. Both priest and king had important economic functions as entrepreneur and banker as well as the more obvious responsibilities for law, order and religious affairs. The buildings emphasise this lack of rigid separatism by apparently combining in some cases several of these functions into one building. The presence of a central authority is further underlined by the appearance of public works, such as water and drainage systems, town planning and town walls which benefited the community as a whole and were carried out by the community. It seems permissible to assume that work of common benefit would be carried out by the community, organised in some cases by the secular head of state and in some cases by the religious leaders.

There is some evidence by the Early Dynastic period for town planning; an interesting example is provided at Khafaje where a residential area was integrated into the planning of the Temple Oval.[48] Too little is known of the layout of Mesopotamian towns in general at this period to be able to generalise, but space was at a premium on any tell site and it is usually assumed that the markets, for example, lay outside the city centres though small "squares" have been observed at Mari, T. Gawra and at T. Chuera. It seems likely that even at this time the cities may have been organised into quarters, a priestly quarter, a merchant quarter, a residential area etc. By the Ur III period these quarters seem to have had a certain autonomy and were organised under "mayors" for purposes of local government within the city wall.[49] A glance at aerial photographs of towns divided as they are into separate tells often by watercourses, reinforces this impression.

The Early Dynastic period probably sees the building of the first city walls,[50] often massive constructions, frequently double, there being an inner and an outer ring of walling strengthened with bastions and entered by triple gates or stairs, where the central arch provided access for wheeled traffic and the smaller flanking passages or stairs for foot traffic.[51] A most elaborate, possibly secret gate, Le Port du Diable, was found at Tello[52] in the thickness of the plano-convex town wall. This consisted of a series of horizontal, vaulted passages linking a number of descending vertical wells, presumably descended by ladder from the top of the wall down, it is presumed, to ground level although unfortunately the base of the wall is below the modern water table so it was not possible to establish conclusively that this was in fact a sally porte. It has even been suggested that it is the shaft of an elaborate, and incidentally, quite atypical tomb.

In a country like Mesopotamia the importance of a civic water supply and municipal drainage system is obviously considerable for health reasons as well as other practical purposes. We have a number of examples of large wells and associated drainage systems most of which seem to be in the temple areas, although a fine well at Adab may be in a secular context.[53] The so-called wells at Fara are more probably silos as traces of grain and date stones were found at the bottom of one. The religious compound at Tello is served by a number of wells and basins connected by channels and drains. The most outstanding is the well of Eannatum on the Maison dés Fruits Tell, built of plano-convex brick laid in the typical herring bone pattern.[54] On the same tell in the so-called Region des Basins were found further cisterns and extensive drainage arrangements together with the remains of heaps of fish, apparently whole fish and not merely discarded bones etc., often in tightly compressed bundles. These two observations suggest the possibility that here we have evidence for a commercial venture in the curing and preservation of fish, possibly for export, as well as for home consumption by temple personnel. This explanation is proposed as an alternative to the view of Mrs Van Buren that these are ritual offerings to the god Ea.[55] Another elaborates series of basins and drains was found on the neighbouring Tell des Piliers, but the excavators seem to have missed any associated walls, finding only the baked brick drains and bitumen floors. Another large cistern was found on the Tell des Tablettes,[56] all the associated channels in this case slope down towards the cistern indicating that it was probably for the collection and retention of rain water. Here again only the bitumened floors and drains were recovered from the associated buildings. Within the ziggurat area at Nippur[57] we have another quite elaborate drainage system, some of it in a remarkable state of preservation. Haynes found what was at that time the earliest true elliptical arch still standing in one of the drainage channels used this time for surface drainage.

Moving on now to the domestic architecture, it is interesting to see whether we can deduce from the meagre evidence at our command any facts about the social life of the time. It might be expected that disparities of wealth and class could be identified and that some indication of the family structure could be deduced from the number and arrangement of rooms within the individual houses. It may also be possible to establish something about the conventions ruling inheritance of property. The basic house plan throughout the period consists of a courtyard or central room flanked on one or more sides by one, two or occasionally three parallel rows of rooms, one room being a large "family" room. This plan was subject to endless modifications due to individual needs and the exigencies of the space available. There has, in the past, been a certain amount of discussion about whether the central court was roofed or not. In some of the larger buildings it obviously was not, the span was too great, but in some of the smaller ones might have been. The evidence from Bismaya however suggests that in the south the "court" was usually open. In the so-called Semitic village[58] Banks reports internal windows which surely suggest that lighting was obtained from an open central court; Hill's arguments for postulating covered courts at T. Asmar[59] do not appear to be entirely convincing even for this rather colder area. Internal windows were found in the Arch House for example. No architectural evidence has been found for roofing methods in these houses, but on analogy with modern houses and with prehistoric sites such as Umm Dabaghayir roofs of mats and mud resting on wooden beams seem entirely plausible. We cannot however assume as has been done in the past that there were no upper storeys.

The evidence for domestic architecture is not extensive and in one instance, Fara, is not well stratified so the Early Dynastic and Agade periods will be treated together, there being no striking typological differences between the two periods, although on the Diyala the tendency seems to be towards greater regularity of street layout and house planning. Let us return first to the question of distribution of wealth and social status. A table compiled by Delougaz and others shows that houses at Khafaje and T. Asmar covered ground areas of anything from between 50 sq.m. to about 300 sq.m., the so-called Arch House in L.IVA exceptionally covered 420 sq.m. This disparity in floor area seems to suggest a considerable unevenness in the distribution of wealth and social standing.[60] Such a deduction is perhaps rather simplistic if one considers a study of a modern village in the area, such as that carried out recently in Asvan in Central Turkey. Here each residential unit can consist of several buildings of very different sizes. For instance an older abandoned house could be used as a store, or stable, while other stores for other commodities, may also be freestanding. This suggests that some of the smaller houses included by Delougaz in his calculations, could in fact have been such ancillary buildings. The calculation of floor areas is also complicated by the possibility of upper storeys over all or part of the ground floor to provide summer quarters or extra living space. These could have been approached by flimsy stairs from a verandah and might have left little trace in the archaeological record. All these factors will have to be borne in mind when trying to assess floor areas, and also when trying to make population estimates based on such assessments. It must also be said that the evidence from Khafaje is atypical in that much of it comes from an area around the Temple Oval which was laid out as part of the complex of which the first Temple Oval was the central feature. This may mean that it has in fact almost the characteristics of a cathedral close and should not be used for generalised deductions. The same objections may be raised with regard to House D at Khafaje and the Scribal Quarter at Nippur where three houses only were partially excavated. However, these observations are borne out by the less extensive information from other sites. At T. Fara[61] the partially destroyed House in IIIa—c is of very considerable size with a courtyard approximately 17 x 22m. Another interesting building occurs in XIIIF where the corner of a building containing large numbers of tablets was found; it has been suggested by the excavator that this was part of a public building of some sort although the stretch of external wall which they found shows us no trace of the buttresses which are often found on public buildings. However, the long narrow room, no. 4 on the plan, may be part of the insulating passage which as we have seen above is also a feature of public buildings. Banks in his work at Adab uncovered many houses, but little information has survived. He does however mention one large house standing in an open square which he dates to the Akkadian period. At Ur in pit F the remains of two buildings were uncovered in Levels E—H, one on either side of a narrow street. The area uncovered was small and the plans fragmentary, but as far as it is possible to say these do not look like the ordinary domestic house plans. Certainly in Levels A–D where only one building is represented something other than a private house is present. The finds in Level A of "numerous lumps of oxide of iron ... with lumps of cuprous oxide" possibly suggest an industrial area, as too does the find of many intact pots laid out in rows[62] in one room of Level E. The area of the pit at its lowest levels was filled with pottery kilns and "wasters" once again suggesting an industrial area. We have seen at Uruk that there are precedents for industrial areas within the ziggurat enclave and that a strong sense of continuity is found in these areas. The one at Uruk covers both Jemdet Nasr and Early Dynastic periods.

Finally at the other end of the social scale we have the huddle of reed huts uncovered at Uruk. These stood together surrounded by their own double enclosure wall, a situation slightly reminiscent of that at Choga Mami at a much earlier date.[63] Dr Oates saw this arrangement as reflecting the social organisation into extended family groups. In any case these reed shacks represent the poorest type of housing we have yet uncovered, and yet one that must have housed a high proportion of the population.

These variations in size taken in conjunction with the great range in the number and richness of grave goods found within burials of the period (ranging as they do at Ur from the opulence of Mes-Kalam-Dug to the plain interments with only one or two pots) point clearly to a considerable disparity in social standing and to an unequal distribution of wealth. There can be little doubt that an aristocracy, better housed and better buried, existed by the Early Dynastic period, though whether it was hereditary, mercantile or priestly we cannot say.

It is interesting to attempt to find evidence for social relations in the architecture, but so far only two small pointers have been recognised. Two houses at T. Asmar show signs of having housed two separate households, the Arch House in Level IVA has two separate, but interconnecting courtyards, each with its own suite of rooms, while in Houses XXXIII/XXXIV[64] the situation is similar, but here each section has its own entrance. It is known from later texts that in certain cases a girl would be sent to the home of her father-in-law and would set up house with the son within the father's house.[65] Such a situation could well be reflected in the architectural features we have just mentioned, but on the other hand these could equally well be explained as belonging to the women's quarter or harem. An analysis of the small finds might suggest the correct answer. It is also interesting to note that a similar situation exists at Khafaje where between Levels 5/4 the commodious House XXXIV is sub-divided, and it appears to house two or possibly three units instead of one. It seems possible that this reflects the custom whereby heritable property was equally divided between all children and sometimes their mother as well.[66] The texts dealing with this situation belong to a considerable later period and we must be cautious about extrapolating backwards. It must be pointed out that various other explanations could fit the observed facts as well as the above suggestion. The fact that the relationship of one room to another is often unclear (if no doorway is recovered) also means that remarks about the size of dwellings must be treated with caution, and any deductions must be recognised as hypotheses and no more.

The practise of interment under the floors of houses is common in the first two-thirds of the Early Dynastic period though by no means universal.[67] The presence of these graves below house floors led to much confusion in the minds of the early excavators and encouraged Koldewey and others to identify whole necropoli, or cities of dead.[68] Frequently the graves were simple pits dug into the floor, but at Khafaje and Kish there is evidence for vaulted mud-brick tombs below the house floors.[69] It is difficult to determine whether the tombs were built when the houses were built, or whether the inhabitants excavated them as the need arose. The fact that some of the tombs utilize the foundation walls of the house as one or two sides of the tombs perhaps suggests contemporaneity, although there is no evidence, such as the keying in of the tomb walls to the house foundations, to prove it. The type of vault is also of considerable importance in determining whether the body could have been inserted later, that is presuming that the tomb was erected when the house was built, and not built for immediate use when required. A corbel-vaulted tomb would be fairly easy to enter from above at a later date while a barrel-vaulted one would not; both types occur at Khafaje. Some of the tombs had doors, but by no means all.[70] A study of the sections showing the relative siting of graves and house floors does not help us as the floor would be broken by the tomb shaft in either case. All in all it seems more likely that the tombs were dug as required and were not a family vault provided with each house and reutilized several times during the lifetime of the house. It is interesting to note in this context that at Khafaje multiple burials were the exception rather than the rule and most tombs seem to have been used once only. It is difficult to understand the criteria which governed the choice of people buried in these tombs; the human remains are of every age and both sexes, but judging from modern comparisons there are not enough remains to account for all the inhabitants of the houses.[71] At Kish no remains of children were found in the tombs, but this could be explained merely by the extreme salinity of the soil which led to the rapid decay of bone. The question then arises, where are the other bodies? It is possible that cremation was practised in some cases; the find of some "burnt" graves[72] in the Royal Cemetery suggests that this rite was used in certain types of burial and there are of course extramural cemeteries of which the Royal Cemetery is the most famous example. The variety of burial rites perhaps emphasises the diverse elements in the population of Mesopotamia by this time.

The techniques used in the construction of the tombs in these extramural cemeteries is similar to that used in the houses although stone is perhaps more commonly employed particularly at the beginning of the period. Most of our information comes from Ur, the extramural tombs at Kish (they post-date the houses among whose ruins they were found,) being few in number, badly ruined and inadequately described. One technique not witnessed in the houses is the use of a coffer dam to build the wall of tombs; the small stones and mortar were poured into the space behind a wooden coffer, rammed down and allowed to set.[73] The Royal graves at Ur bear witness to a command of most of the techniques of roofing; PG 777 has a corbelled vault and a barrel-vaulted passage; PG 779 has two small chambers with ring domes; the door of PG 789 has a true arch and PG 1050 has a flat roof "of native type".[74]

This then completes our survey of the architectural remains from Sumer and Akkad. Some of the observed features may be explained by the ecological background—for example the over-whelming prevalence of mud-brick[75]—some by the social conditions, though these tentative deductions are merely untested "models" and as such serve little purpose other than to suggest possible future fields of research, and some by diffusion and cultural interactions. With this possibility in mind we wish next to survey the evidence from the geographical area to the North of Baghdad to determine if possible the influence of one area upon the other.

NOTES

[1] Binford and Binford (eds.), *New perspectives in Archaeology*, passim, esp. J.Deetz, *Inference of residence and descent rules from archaeological data*, p. 41., also F.Hole on the evidence from Deh Luran: newly excavated Middle East data is used in an attempt to deduce social organisation.

[2] For the model of a weaving shed, H.E.Winlock, *Models of daily life in Ancient Egypt*, pls. 25, 26 and 27.

[3] For a modern example of this type of cottage industry, cf. S.M.Salim, *Marsh dwellers of the Euphrates Delta*, p. 108—109.

[4] An exception is the site partially excavated by H.Wright and described in "The administration of rural production in an early Mesopotamian town."

[5] At Tell Asmar, plano-convex bricks do not occur until Archaic IV although Archaic I—IV are all dated by the excavator to E.D.I. Conversely plano-convex bricks occur in private houses at Nippur in an Agade context. McCown and Haines, *Nippur* I. For a general discussion, cf. P.Delougaz, 'Plano-convex bricks and the method of their employ-ment', *S.A.O.C.*, no. 7, Chicago.

[6] Cf. *Archaeology* 21, no. 4; for a brief description, p. 304.

[7] *U.V.B.* IX, p. 7. Lenzen suggests that Ziggurat I may have been Agade in date.

[8] P.Delougaz, *P.S.T.*, pls. V and VI.

40

9   Hansen and Dales, *Archaeology* XV, no. 2; S.Lloyd, *J.N.E.S.* II.2, pl. IV.

10 *P.S.T.*, pl. 17 for the development of the Small temple and pl. 16 for the last phase of the Nintu temple; also pp. 80—104. For the Small Single Shrine, fig. 105, p. 114.

11 *P.S.T.*, pl. 23 for the development of the Single Shrine Abu temple.

12 Hansen and Dale, *Archaeology* XV, no. 2 and V.E.Crawford, *Archaeology* XII, no. 1.

13 For the Construction Inférieure, A.Parrot, *Telloh*, fig. 13, p. 55, and for the shrine of Ur-Nanshe, pl. 15, p. 62.

14 *P.S.T.*, pl. 22.

15 *P.S.T.*, pls. 2—12.

16 *P.S.T.*, pl. 12.

17 P.Delougaz, *The Temple Oval.* passim. For the Ubaid temple; Hall & Woolley, *Al Ubaid*, and P.Delougaz in *Iraq* V. 'A short investigation of the temple at Al Ubaid;' for the Al Hibba temple, V.E.Crawford in *Expedition* 14, no. 2 and D.Hansen in *Artibus Asiae* XXXII, no. 4, p. 243.

18 For a summary of work on the Barbar temple, G.Bibby, *Looking for Dilmun.* More detailed articles have appeared in *Kuml* 1970 and by P.Mortensen in *Artibus asiae* XXXIII, no. 4, p. 299—302.

19 The Tummal inscriptions are published by E.Sollberger in *J.C.S.* XVI, p. 40.

20 Banks, *Bismaya*, p. 237—247.

21 McCown and Haines, *op. cit.*, p. 3.

22 P.R.S.Moorey in *Iraq* XXVII, pt. I, p. 29. 'A reconsideration of the excavations at Tell Inghara.'

23 C.L.Woolley, *Ur* V, p. 11—23; P.N.Weadock, 'The Giparu at Ur', in *Iraq* XXXVII, pt. 2, p. 101.

24 For the most complete plan of the 'Enceinte sacrée' at Mari, A.Parrot in *Syria* XLVI, p. 196, fig. 3. The Archaic Temple is not nearly so imposing in concept as the 'Enceinte Sacrée, but the concept of a shrine within a much larger, multi-purpose building appears to be common to all three buildings. For the Shara temple, P.Delougaz, *P.S.T.*, fig. 203.

25 *P.S.T.*, p. 203—204.

26 McCown and Haines, *op. cit.*, p. 3; V.E.Crawford, *op. cit.*, p. 79.

27 Banks, *Bismaya*, p. 235.

28 For discussion of the history, purpose, and development of the ziggurat, cf. H.Lenzen, *Die Entwicklung der Ziggurat*, and P.Amiet in *La Glyptique archaïque Mésopotamienne*, p. 181ff. for the view that there

were no ziggurats in the E.D. period. Also P.R.S.Moorey in *Iraq* XXVIII, pt. 1, p. 27.

[29] Cf. Moorey's reappraisal of the Kish excavations in *Iraq* XXVII, pt. 1, p. 25.

[30] C.S.Fisher, *Excavations at Nippur*, p. 11 and H.Hilprecht, *Explorations in Bible Lands*, p. 453.

[31] Banks, *Bismaya*, p. 244, and an inadequate plan on p. 235.

[32] A.Parrot, *Telloh*, p. 65 and A.Parrot, *Ziggurats*, p. 148.

[33] C.L.Woolley, *Ur* V, pp. 5–6 and pl. 67.

[34] For a summary of the evidence, cf. Elliot's *Graphic Analysis*, and *U.V.B.* IX and X, taf. 5. For the E.D. II dating of Eanna II, *U.V.B.* II, p. 27–28 and Abb. 13. For the industrial area, *U.V.B.* XVI, p. 9–10, and for descriptions of courtyard with ? offering stands *U.V.B.* XVIII, p. 11, taf. 31, and *U.V.B.* XIX, p. 15, taf. 47. This area is possibly linked to a badly ruined road and gateway, *U.V.B.* XVII, p. 16 and taf. 29. Another gateway in sq. Na XVI.3 which was established in the J.N. period and rebuilt in plano-convex bricks is described in *U.V.B.* XVII, p. 12. The problem of whether or not to include the temples of Eanna IV in this survey of third millennium architecture is a difficult one. Although the pottery has J.N. affinities, there is a complete architectural break between levels IV–III and none of the plans of 1.IV reoccur. *U.V.B.* VII, p. 9 and VIII, p. 8–9. On the other hand, features typical of Eanna II–1.2, such as the high platform and the Opferstatten occur for the first time in L.III. Elliot, *op. cit.* would support the placing of the L.IV tablets in a pre-Jemdet Nasr context and it is generally agreed that they cannot be the first and most primitive attempts at writing. Cf. also Behnam al Soof, 'Relevance of the Diyala sequence to S. Mesopotamian sites', *Iraq* XXIX, p. 133.

[35] For the pavement of Naram-Sin, cf. Hilprecht, *op. cit.*, diagram, p. 394, and for the enclosure wall, C.S.Fisher, *op. cit.*, p. 29.

[36] For the 'Curse of Agade', cf. A.Falkenstein in *Z.F.A.* 57, p. 43.

[37] Banks, *Bismaya*, p. 236.

[38] See the texts from Lagash and the cone of Urukagina quoted by S.N.Kramer in *The Sumerians*, Appendix C., p. 318.

[39] E.Mackay, *A Sumerian palace and the A cemetery at Kish*. The doorway to the palace is described on p. 92.

[40] P.R.S.Moorey, 'The plano-convex brick building at Kish', *Iraq* XXVI, pt. 2, p. 83 and plan on pl. XXI.

[41] F.Safar, *Sumer* VI, fig. 3.

[42] Cf. plan in *Sumer* XIV, Arabic section, also S.A.Rashid in *Sumer* XIX for a summary in German.

[43] *U.V.B.* XXIII, p. 24 and taf. 29. Also *Archaeology* 19, no. 1, p. 54.

[44] C.L.Woolley, *Ur* IV, p. 80, pls. 70 and 71, IIB. The evidence from pit F is too incomplete to allow any interpretation, pls. 74 and 75.

[45] Delougaz *et al. PHD*, p. 183—185, and p. 196—198 and pl. 36.

[46] Delougaz *et al. PHD*, p. 186—198 and pl. 37, also pl. 20 and p. 23.

[47] G.Cros, *Nouvelles fouilles de Tello*, pl. F, p. 229.

[48] Delougaz *et al. PHD*, p. 9. There is some evidence for town planning even earlier than the Ubaid period. Recent excavations at Tell es Sawwan show an elaborate ditch and buttressed wall surrounding the settlement in the Samarra period, cf. Behnam Abu al-Soof, 'Tell es Sawwan, 4th season,' in *Sumer* XXIV, 1968, p. 4.

[49] Cf. for example the tablet showing the plan of Nippur c.1500 B.C. A good photograph in McCown and Haines, *Nippur* I, pl. 4 and also Woolley's discussion of the private houses excavated at Ur. *Excavations at Ur*, p. 174. For the internal organisation of the city, A.L.Oppenheim, *Ancient Mesopotamia*, p. 115—117 and Middle Eastern Cities, ed. Lapidus, esp. chapters by Oppenheim and Adams.

[50] For the wall at Nippur, C.S.Fisher, *Excavations at Nippur*, p. 21—28; Uruk wall, *U.V.B.* VII, p. 42, *U.V.B* VIII, pls. 1—4; Adab wall, Banks, *Bismaya*, p. 335; Khafaje and T.Asmar walls, *PHD*, p. 24 and 257; Lagash wall, Cros, *op. cit.*, p. 63.

[51] Cf. Fisher, *op. cit.*, p. 21—28 for a description of the gateway at Nippur. A similar gateway of plano-convex bricks was also excavated at Abu Shahrein by J.E.Taylor, cf. *Journal of the Royal Asiatic Society* XV, p. 409.

[52] G.Cros, *op. cit.*, p. 63ff.

[53] For a photograph of the silo at Fara Mus., J.Penn, Vol. XXII, nos. 3—4, pl. V. For the well at Adab, Banks, *Bismaya*, p. 331.

[54] For Eannatum's well, A.Parrot, *Tello*, p. 62 and plan 16, p. 64.

[55] E.D.Van Buren, 'Places of sacrifice', *Iraq* XIV, p. 77. There is evidence for pre-Sargonid smoking, drying, and salting of fish in considerable quantities and also for its storage in 'fish-houses' by the temples, but there is no direct evidence for foreign trade. Cf. E.Salonen, *Die fischerei in alten Mesopotamien*. In a text known as 'The home of the Fish', there is a damaged line which refers to merchants doing something to or with fish. M.Civil, 'The Home of the Fish', in *Iraq* XXIII, line 109; also H.E.W.Crawford, 'Mesopotamia's invisible exports', *World Archaeology* 5.2, p. 232.

[56] *Tell des Piliers.* Cros, *op. cit.*, p. 101; *Tell des Tablettes*, Cros, *op. cit.*, p. 252.

[57] H.Hilprecht, *Explorations in Bible Lands*, p. 394 and pl. facing p. 399.

[58] Banks, *op. cit.*, p. 303 and plan p. 304.

[59] Delougaz *et al. PHD*, p. 143–151.

[60] Delougaz, *PHD*, table II facing p. 277 and *Anatolian Studies* XXIII, 1973, p. 245.

[61] E.Heinrich and W.Andrae, *Fara 1902/3*, p. 12 and taf. 5 and for XIIIf, p. 14, abb. 12.

[62] Banks, *op. cit.*, p. 300–304, pl. 304. Also C.L.Woolley, *Ur* IV, pls. 74–75 and pp. 56–65.

[63] For a description of these houses, *U.V.B.* X, pl. II and p. 17. For the bayt at Choga Mami, J.Oates in *Iraq* XXXI, p. 143.

[64] Delougaz *et al. PHD*, pl. 28, and for the development of the Arch house, pl. 33.

[65] Driver and Miles, *The Babylonian Laws. Legal commentary*, p. 250.

[66] For a plan of the house in question, cf. Delougaz, *PHD*, pl. 8, house XXXIV; pl. 10, house XL. For the legal aspect, cf. Driver and Miles, *op. cit.*, pp. 324–341 and A.Falkenstein, *Die Neusumerischen Gerichtsurkunden*, p. 113.

[67] The proportion of vaulted tombs at Khafaje falls off sharply in the E.D. III, (levels 1, 2, 3.). Cf. Delougaz, *PHD*, table 1, p. 134ff. Only one grave was found under the E.D. III and proto-imperial houses at T. Asmar, *PHD*, p. 171.

[68] Koldewey in *Z.f.A.* II, 1887, p. 403ff. For a summary in English, Hilprecht, *op. cit.*, p. 284–286.

[69] For the graves at Khafaje, Delougaz, *PHD* p. 58ff. For Y cemetery at Kish, L.C.Watelin, *Kish* IV, Chapter II. The A cemetery produced no built tombs.

[70] Delougaz, *PHD*, pl. 59D and pl. 60A for a tomb with a door.

[71] H.Wright, *op. cit.*, quotes figures for population density. Also while some houses contain 6, 7 or even more graves, others contain only one or sometimes none at all. One grave at Khafaje, no. 133, contained the remains of five individuals and the fragmentary condition of some of the bodies may indicate re-utilization of the tomb.

[72] C.L.Woolley, *Ur. The Royal Cemetery*, p. 226.

[73] Woolley, *op. cit.*, p. 229.

[74] Woolley, *op. cit.*, p. 232–236.

[75] For the most comprehensive description of the techniques employed in the making of mud brick, cf. P.Delougaz, *SAOC*, no. 7, *passim.*

CHAPTER III

Architecture in the Jazirah

Although there is plenty of evidence for the occupation of sites in North Mesopotamia at a period equivalent to the Early Dynastic period in the South, there is a paucity, as in the South, of well stratified material. Most of the evidence comes from excavations which fall far short of modern requirements of accuracy, observation and recording. One of the latest examples of this is provided by the very important German excavations at T. Chuera in N. Syria where the relationship of one building to another is nowhere defined by stratification or illustrated by sections. It is to be hoped that this will be remedied when the final report is published. In the meantime the architectural sequence from this site, which shows many new and intriguing features, is of less use to us than might have been hoped, because the chronological sequence of the various monuments is often in doubt as is their absolute dating. As in the South the evidence is again heavily weighted towards monumental architecture with "temples" and "palaces" outnumbering ordinary houses or industrial buildings.

The building material in the North is still primarily mud-brick although the ubiquitous plano-convex brick of the South is only rarely found north of Baghdad. There are plano-convex bricks at Braq in the fragmentary temple which overlies the Eye Temples, at T.Hawa north of the Jebel Sinjar, and at T. Jidle on the Balikh river.[1] It would be tempting to deduce that the sites which produce plano-convex bricks represent actual occupation by Sumerian colonies, planted perhaps by a Sumerian conqueror on his way to save the merchants of Purushkanda or wash his weapons in the upper sea, while the sites which merely produce buildings and artefacts in the Sumerian style are reflecting the influence, political religious and artistic, of the South without implying anything more than the contacts provided by trade and "international politics". Until our present evidence is strengthened by textual material this must remain no more than speculation, however attractive it may sound. Stone was more widely used for foundations etc. in the North merely because it was more freely available, for example at T. Chuera and T. Taya. At both these sites mud-brick superstructures were used as well. The builders of the North seem to have had as much technical skill as their southern counterparts although numerically the examples of their work are fewer. Gawra VIIIa produced examples of the true arch in what is probably an Early Dynastic I/II context,[2] while the tombs underlying Ishtar Temple C at Mari and dating to about the same period or slightly earlier are corbel-vaulted;[3] corbelling is of course also attested from considerably earlier periods. The fine decoration of pilasters and recesses which adorns the courtyards of some of the buildings, for example that of the temple of Ninnizaza at Mari,[4] also demonstrates a considerable technical facility as does the discovery of drains on some sites still with their vaulting intact after four thousand years or more.

Even from these brief remarks it will be seen that it is an over-simplification to regard the North as a poor sister of the Sumerian South. It is true however that in the Early Dynastic period the area shows a lack of standardisation in religious architecture as does the South, which perhaps reflects the fragmented nature of the political situation; no unifying central authority can be detected in the area as a whole.[5] Of the temple plans known in the South types C, Bipartite, and E, Temple Ovals, are unknown in the North. There is one example at T. Braq of Type A, Tripartite, and one at T. Chuera of Type B, the Single Room Temple; two new types occur, Type G, the Megaron, and H, the Flanked Altar type.

The first Group, A, is represented by the Jemdet Nasr Eye Temple at T. Braq, a slightly asymmetrical version of the classic tripartite plan;[6] Group B, by a building from T. Chuera, a rectangular shrine with the entrance in the long side; it lies south of the North Anten Temple and the "Artisan" quarter.[7] The shrine lies below the levels containing Nuzi sherds and as it seems unrelated to the North Temple, of tentatively Early Dynastic date, may well belong to the end of the third millennium. Third is Group D which appears to be modelled on the house plans then in vogue and is ilustrated by two examples from Mari. Parrot points out that the temple of Ninnizaza and the temple of Ishtarat[8] are based on the ordinary house plan with a central court surrounded by the living quarters. At this site there is no trace of a second storey although the house models suggest that this was sometimes found. The temple of Ninnizaza is slightly irregular in plan as it is fitted into the angle formed by two roads. Its most notable feature is a finely decorated courtyard as mentioned above, which in a second phase of occupation has the unusual feature of a standing stone or obelisk in the centre of the court. The largest room, which runs the whole width of the building and has two doors onto the central court, has all the usual temple fittings of altar, benches and "barcasses". The temple of Ishtarat must be somewhat later than the above in date as it abuts onto it, but in no case are the two walls bonded into each other. The excavated area appears to be only part of a larger building complex and the wing which we have follows the house plan of a normal dwelling with the addition of a monumental entrance. The Enceinte Sacrée, also in effect a House Plan temple will be fully discussed later in the chapter when the PP[1] palace is described.

Ishtar temples H and G[9] at Assur also seem to be part of a House Plan temple with the cella giving onto a main courtyard which was surrounded on two remaining sides with what appear to be service rooms. The finds from H and G form a homogeneous group of Early Dynastic date and the Akkadian head from the courtyard in Level G is now thought to be intrusive. The ivory figure of a woman from Level G has close parallels with the figure from the PP[1] palace at Mari and the statuary is of a typical Early Dynastic variety. In common with other Early Dynastic temples, Temple G was pillaged and burnt.

Group F is a miscellaneous group which contains a variety of fragmentary or poorly understood plans as well as the Ishtar Temple at Mari which at the moment has no counterpart elsewhere, with its pillared court and slightly trapexoidal cella.[10]

Several examples of the Megaron plan, Group G, are known from T. Chuera but unfortunately, as mentioned above, the dating criteria are not entirely satisfactory. The "Aussenbau complex"[11] with one megaron temple is almost certainly later than the Early

Dynastic period, but the Northern Temple with its apsidal end wall behind the presumed site of the podium finds a parallel in the partially destroyed megarons of Troy Ia and would agree with an Early Dynastic date.[12] The association of this temple with a pottery producing area would also agree with the evidence for industrial complexes closely associated with temples in the Jemdet Nasr and Early Dynastic phases at Uruk. The small finds from the North Temple are mostly figurines and models of a type which have a fairly long life in Mesopotamia and therefore are not a great deal of help in trying to establish a precise date.

The third temple of the Megaron type, Moortgat's Kleiner Anten Temple,[13] is built on an earlier temple of different design; this earlier plan has a single room shrine with an anteroom and various service areas of irregular shape; the temple is associated in its second and third phases with some characteristically Sumerian statuary of the later Early Dynastic period.[14] This factor would seem to place the second and third phases of the Kleiner Anten Temple in the later part of the Early Dynastic period, but Agade pottery from Level 1 suggests that the temple survived into this period. It would seem on the evidence from T. Chuera that the Megaron style of temple was probably known in North Syria from the beginning of the Early Dynastic period, if we accept the North Temple as being early, and that it continued in favour into the second millennium if not later, on the evidence of the Aussenbau Anten Temple.

The Eastern and West Temples in Level VIII at T. Gawra also show evidence of the Megaron plan in that they both have deep porches with the entrance on the short side of the cella opposite the site of the altar; each of them has additional rooms flanking the cella so that in effect they are combining the traditional tripartite temple plan, our type A, of the later prehistoric period in Sumer with the Megaron plan from the West and represent an interesting fusion of cultures.[15] On the other hand, the possibility that these two temples really represent a local modification of the old southern Tripartite Plan, without any western influences, cannot be dismissed out of hand.

Another group of temple plans, our type H, or Flanked Altar type, seems to provide an interesting architectural sequence. The first example is the so-called "House" in Level II at Grai Resh.[16] There is no unambiguous evidence for accepting this as a shrine, but the careful workmanship and the presence of two niches in the north wall of the large central room, or court, are pointers in this direction; the flanking service rooms almost give it the air of a tripartite temple plan. The building also has a close resemblance to an Uruk building at T. eth Thalathat which both the excavators and Professor Mallowan accept as a temple[17] although again the case is perhaps arguable. The T. eth Thalathat building has an "altar" at one end of the main room or court, but the niches are absent and it is interesting to note that the treatment of the altar in the tripartite temple is often similar, with niches flanking the main altar, and to speculate on the relationship of one plan to the other. The second link in the chain of development is provided by the Northern Temple at T. Gawra which is at least unambiguously a shrine.[18] It is rectangular with two niches on one of the short walls of the main chamber, this time the western wall, and the entrance lies on the long wall as at Grai Resh. Its internal length is c.9m. as is that of the "house" at Grai Resh and that of the shrine at T. Taya[19] which provides a third and later example of the same type of shrine. At T. Taya however the niches have become two small rooms, one on either side of the podium. Their usage is not clear, but they perhaps served much the same purpose as a modern vestry. The find in one of them of hundreds of blue frit beads might suggest the storing of some sort of ceremonial garments or ornaments, either for the priest or for the statue of the god.[20]

The building at Grai Resh is associated with late Uruk pottery and underlies plain Nineveh V ware which is now usually considered later than the painted variety; a date in the Jemdet Nasr period is suggested, and perhaps towards the end of that period as the typical Nineveh V chalice is already present although there is apparently no painted ware. The Northern Temple at T. Gawra survives throughout the whole of Level VIII which brings us into the Early Dynastic period. The shrine at T. Taya has to be dated more by inference than by associated finds, but the excavator puts it in the Early Dynastic period and it can hardly be pushed back earlier than this. We have then, tentatively, examples of this admittedly very simple plan from the late Uruk period to the Agade period as the Taya shrine survives into this period. If the "shrine" at T. eth Thalathat is also accepted as being in the same tradition the plan is taken one step further back. It is interesting to note that the plan seems to survive into the second millennium with the building at Mari of the Dagan temple actually within the mass of the ziggurat. It is laid out in almost the same way as the T. Taya shrine, but the entrance is now opposite the podium which is again flanked by two small rooms, so that there is a direct axis, instead of a bent axis approach.[21]

Finally we come back to the miscellaneous group, Group F. Mari has produced fragmentary remains of several other Early Dynastic temples some of which seem to have been devastated at the end of that period, possibly by Sargon, and never rebuilt. Others have been built over at a later date so that recovery of earlier plans is difficult. Three temples are clustered round the great ziggurat, one face of which has been shown to be Early Dynastic with the typical pilaster and recess decoration. It was heavily restored after this and the rest of the Early Dynastic building has not been traced.[22] The pre-Sargonid temple of Dagan,[23] predecessor of later temples, although on a slightly different site, has a poorly understood plan which appears to be divided into two sections, one obviously the public and ceremonial part with large courts, and the second being internally subdivided by a curving passage slightly reminiscent of the internal arrangements of the Early Dynastic palaces in the South. Judging from the small finds, this area appears to be the living quarters, stores, etc., of the priestesses of Dagan; the finds include a charming mosaic showing the priestesses with their spindles busy at their work.[24] It is interesting to note that the principle that male gods should be served by priestesses still seems to hold good. Parrot regards this temple as one of the most significant finds at Mari.

Two other temples closely associated with the ziggurat and with each other are those of Shamash[25] and Ninhursag.[26] The plans of both are fragmentary; the temple of Shamash has produced one unusual, and at the moment unexplained feature, a great pit, Parrot's "Grande Fosse". Is it possible that this could be the shaft of a tomb the chamber of which has not yet been reached? Both these temples appear to have survived into the Agade period. As noted above, the Ishtar temple is also placed somewhat arbitrarily in this group as its trapezoidal cella and pillared court are unique.

Leaving Mari, another unclassifiable temple comes from Gawra VIII a—c.[27] In these levels the so-called Central Shrine shows a number of unusual features and indeed is only taken as a shrine because of the crenellated facade, a decoration which is usually reserved for religious buildings. The two rooms which flank the porch are distinguished by small, almost triangular windows, placed at the back of a niche. This type of window is well known on the model house type of offering stand usually dated to the Early Dynastic period.[28] No altar or podium was found and the entrance, through a porch, was on one of the long walls of the rectangular main room.

The last shrine to be mentioned in this context is that excavated by Professor S.Lloyd at T. Khoshi.[29] He seems content to accept this small room in the thickness of the town wall as a religious building when a guardroom would be more appropriate to its situation. However, in Level I there would appear to be a shrine in the same position, so perhaps we should accept Level II as a shrine as well, though with slight reservations. Level II is associated with incised and plain pottery of Nineveh V type.

As in the South, the remains of the Agade period are comparatively scarce and ill-preserved. Once again this is perhaps to be attributed to the political uncertainty and poverty which followed the fall of the Sargonid empire rather than to the depredations of the Agade kings themselves. As any field archaeologist knows, there is nothing like a good catastrophe, fire or sack for preserving the archaeological evidence, while the levels which yield least are those which are gradually depopulated and allowed to decay and crumble due to poverty, unsettled political conditions, a breakdown in central administration or a hundred other causes. It is reasonable to suppose that these conditions prevailed in North Mesopotamia from possibly as early as the death of Naram-Sin; he was already engaged in fighting off the Lullubi and other hill tribes and it is perhaps their activities, rather than the destruction wrought by Akkadian conquerors, which have produced this situation. In the field of religious building there are however some exceptions to this observation, and one of them is provided by T. Chuera which perhaps lay to the west of the area affected by the troubles of the late and post-Sargonid periods. It must be remembered that the dating is extremely tentative. It will be recalled that the Aussenbau Anten Tempel of Type G was considered to be Agade or later. Moortgat dates the temple to the Agade period and it is suggested that it was founded at this time and continued in use till considerably later, as two phases of building are mentioned and the pottery is consistent with an Agade-Ur III dating.[30] In the South the Bit Akitu which has obvious parallels with the Aussenbau complex is known from as early as the third millennium.

There is also one example of the second new type of temple mentioned in this chapter, Type H, the rectangular cella with two niches or small rooms, one on either side of the podium. The shrine at T. Taya[31] remained in use with its plan apparently unchanged through two sub-phases Levels VII and VIII in spite of a destruction and sack at the end of Level VIII which again reflects the uncertain political conditions obtaining by the middle of the Agade period.

Moving on to Mari, the evidence is again meagre in the extreme. The Ninnizaza and Ishtarat temples were not rebuilt after they and the palace had been sacked, possibly by Sargon himself. The Enceinte Sacrée within the palace was however rebuilt and this reconstruction was dated by Parrot to the Ur III period,[32] but may perhaps be a little earlier as there is a certain continuity of plan; the altar in the cella is built on top of the earlier one. This argues against the longer abandonment of the site and the reconstruction probably took place earlier. Building certainly continued at Mari during the Agade period, although the remains are on the whole fragmentary. The Ninhursag[33] temple was rebuilt with a double shrine and there is some evidence for an Agade level at the Shamash temple. An Agade level at the Dagan temple has not yet been identified and at the site of the Ishtar temple the period is represented only by a few stray small finds. There is a somewhat puzzling feature named Les Temples Inférieurs close to the ziggurat, where a fine monumental entrance leads into a courtyard in which an altar, with two statue bases in situ on it, was found. The rest of the plan is unclear but Parrot tentatively dates the complex to the Agade period.[34] At Assur, the Ishtar temple there[35] was also destroyed at the end of the Early Dynastic period and the Agade level F is remarkable only for the paucity of its remains and for the fact that the walls are based on stone footings for the first time.

Finally there is the temple built by Manishtusu of Akkad at Assur which is known only from an inscription, no actual remains have been found.

We have noted that in the South the ziggurat was already a feature of religious building by the end of the Early Dynastic period, but leaving aside the enigmatic Steinbauen at T. Chuera, Mari is the only site in the North which has produced a ziggurat that appears to go back to the Early Dynastic period. The Steinbauen cannot even be classed as buildings on present evidence; they are massive stone-built constructions one of which, Steinbau III, has a finely built stair on the east side which starts from a mud-brick platform below the level of the Steinbau wall. It is not even clear whether the area enclosed by the heavy stone wall was a solid mass of material or if it was subdivided by walls. The dating of these three puzzling monuments is also uncertain. Stainbau I is said to be earlier than the funerary complex which adjoins it and in the lowest level of which was found a sealing of Early Dynastic II date. However the pottery associated with Steinbau I is said to be Akkadian so it is probably safer in the absence of any sections to assign an Akkadian date to the construction. Steinbau II which lies east of I but unconnected with it stratigraphically has no date assigned to it; lastly Moortgat states that Steinbau III is earlier than Steinbau I and on the basis of parallels between the pottery and that from the later levels of the Kleiner Anten Tempel dates Steinbau III to the Early Dynastic period.[36] Moortgat tentatively describes these curious structures as stone ziggurats; the association of one of them with a funerary complex certainly suggests that they were religious in purpose, but graves are not essentially associated with ziggurats in Mesopotamia and we should perhaps regard them more in the light of gigantic memorials to the dead.

Turning now to the public buildings in the Early Dynastic period which are not overtly religious, Mari has produced the magnificent palaces PP[1] and 2.[37] Here again the basic plan is the same as in the South and several autonomous units are put together to provide a larger building. The most interesting feature of this palace is the discovery within it of a self-contained religious enclave, isolated on three sides by a passage and called by Parrot the "Enceinte Sacrée"; the courtyard of the Enceinte in the earlier phase of the palace is decorated with painted pilasters in low relief; this type of decoration characterises the older of the two palaces. The younger palace PP1 was savagely destroyed, pillaged and burnt. The fragmentary small finds are of typically Early Dynastic type and include the famous bead inscribed with the name of Mes-anne-padda which was found buried in the courtyard. The destruction is usually attributed to either Lugal-zagesi or Sargon himself. The Enceinte Sacrée was rebuilt after the holocaust, but Parrot is inclined to date that rebuilding to the Ur III period.[38] Some continuity of plan is demonstrated so perhaps the rebuilding should be dated a little earlier, possibly in the later Sargonid period. The presence of a religious enclave within what appears to be a ruler's palace raises interesting speculations about the role of the king as high priest, or of the high priest as king, and indeed about the admissibility of the terms "religious" and "secular" in a third millennium context. This is the only building in the North which can with some certainty be called a palace, though various others exist which possibly fall into this category.

There are three other public buildings of a secular nature from T. Gawra Level VIII. The first in VIIIc is described by Speiser as being possibly a priest's house mainly because it backs onto the central temple, but the thick walls coupled with a typical layout and the apparent absence of doors perhaps indicate that it was a municipal granary or storehouse, the forerunner of the storage unit in the same area in Level VIIIb.[39] The fact that the floors of the rooms were covered with a thin layer of bitumen, presumably to prevent rising damp, also suggests the presence of perishable goods of some sort. The second structure belongs to Level VIIIa and faces the central shrine.[40] The layout of the building on a tripartite plan would in other situations immediately suggest a religious building, but in Gawra where there is already a plethora of temples it is perhaps more satisfactory to accept Speiser's interpretation of it as a dwelling. The third building is more correctly a complex of buildings containing an arched, vaulted hall, a courtyard and a deep liwan or porch giving onto what was presumably a living room of some sort with various subsidiary rooms opening off it.[41] It is in what Speiser calls the New Quarter of the town built in VIIIa and is perhaps the official residence of an important official, the hall being a meeting place, law court, or banqueting hall, and the liwan and its adjacent rooms being the private living quarters.

Part of a house was excavated under the later Sin-Shamash temple at Assur and is dated to the Agade period by Preusser on the evidence of the pottery.[42] It is interesting in that part of two courts with adjacent rooms were excavated and the nearest parallel is that of the Naram-Sin palace at T. Braq; although the Assur building is on a much less grandiose scale than the Braq one, it is almost certainly something larger than a mere private house.

The palace, or more correctly barracks-cum-depot at Braq[43] with its four courtyards, is an excellent example of practical empire building and seems almost Roman in conception with its regular plan, stamped bricks, right angled corners and general air of efficiency. The so-called ER site at Braq[44] has yielded another group of small rooms which also look like a storage area. The CH site[45] on the other hand seems to have been a residential quarter although no complete house plans were recovered. At Chagar Bazar Mallowan attributes Level 4 to the Sargonid period and although the remains for Level 5 were fragmentary, Level 4 produced the plan of a street[46] to the south of which lay a small rectangular building with a little porch, which is tentatively identified as a shrine although no distinctive features were found in the room itself. The other side of the street is occupied by a few rooms obviously part of a large and fairly elaborate building. On comparing the plan of this level with the plan of the succeeding Level 3 on the one hand, and with the palaces of Early Dynastic date, especially that at Mari, on the other, one is tempted to suggest that the street, 2 on the plan, is in fact a passage and all the rooms are part of the same large complex. A passage isolating the Enceinte Sacrée at Mari is analogous in appearance.

In dealing with the evidence from the South it was suggested that the presence of a central authority could be deduced not only from the presence of these large buildings but also from the indications of town planning, town defences and public works such as drainage and water supply. Some evidence for the deliberate planning of towns is found at Mari, T. Chuera, T. Taya and T. Gawra; at Mari a small area of the pre-Sargonid town was excavated, bringing to light an interesting feature. This is a small, somewhat irregular square with pillars round the perimeter apparently forming an arcade under which it is not hard to imagine a market, a cafe, and all the other elements of everyday life in a town.[47] Two small open squares also appear on the plan of the houses at T. Chuera, one of which seems to have a number of "fittings" whose nature is not clear.[48] Such a feature is unusual in that space in tell towns is usually at such a premium that town planning allows for few open areas, and markets etc. often seen to have been held outside the town gates, presumably on the open ground at the foot of the tell.[49] Within the walls the houses usually seem to jostle against each other, frequently so close together that the unbroken line presented by their backs formed a second line of defence behind the town wall.[50]

It is interesting to note that the temple of Ninnizaza at Mari was forced by the pre-existing street plan into an irregular quadrilateral. The road apparently could not be re-routed to accommodate a more regularly shaped building. Unlike the South, there is very little evidence for industrial activity within the towns. There are only two possibly industrial areas, an area adjacent to the North Temple at T. Chuera which seems to have been the centre of a pottery workshop producing figurines as well as pots and a flint working area outside the town at T. Taya.

Agade levels have been explored at T. Gawra and at T. Taya. T. Gawra Level VI[52] marks a complete rebuilding and reorganisation of the available space and must have been centrally planned. The buildings, all on stone foundations, were laid out round a small central square from which streets radiated out to provide access to the two town gates and circulation between the houses. The house plans are very irregular and do not show the grouping round a central court characteristic of other sites; also in contrast to Level VIII there is no obviously religious building. A row of rooms set side by side round the edge of the mound with their backs facing outwards to form an inner defensive wall were found, also traces of a second wall lower down the slopes of the mound. There is some evidence for a stone-based watch tower flanking the eastern gateway (room 607 on Plan VII). Further, presumably unprotected, houses lay at the foot of the mount as at T. Taya where a grid plan of streets is evident.

One of the features of the Early Dynastic period in the South is the recognition of massive town walls which became of strategic importance with the increase in political consciousness and the increase in wealth which went hand in hand with the rise in the standard of living and dying. The North has produced a number of fortified sites of which T. Taya provides the most recent example. Here there were in effect three fortified enclosures of which the most heavily guarded was the citadel which contained a shrine, possibly a second one, and probably in the early phases one or more important houses. The citadel wall which was circular and strengthened by basions, apparently at regular intervals, is built on a footing of stone about 3m. high above which is a layer of sherds set in mud mortar, presumably for drainage, and above this again a superstructure of mud-brick. At the foot of the citadel was part of the town, which in turn was surrounded by an approximately oval enclosure wall with at least one strengthening tower. Onto this oval enclosure abutted a rectangular one which had a single range of rooms along its inner face; these have a slightly military air, unless they represent a storage area. Not all the houses of the town lay within these three walls; some lay on the other side of the stream and were apparently unprotected.[53] In Level VII an interesting development was noted in the presence of a glacis for the first time outside the citadel wall. The gateway into the citadel is an impressive affair with a vaulted passage and guardroom and stairs leading up onto the ramparts. Massive walls are also known from Nuzi, T. Jidle, T. Khoshi and Grai Resh although their dating is not always very secure.[54] A solidly built double wall was found at T. Chuera; as far as it is possible to tell from the published plans, this encircled the whole of the built-up area, but no indication of its date is given.[55] From the placing of the Aussenbau complex almost in line with the point on the circumference where today the mouth of the wadi, which divides the site in two, debouches it is reasonable to postulate a town gate at this point. It is hard to believe that towns of the strategic and political importance of Mari and Assur should not have been fortified even though the walls have not been excavated. The entrance to the Ishtar Temple G at Assur seems to be below one of the later gates into the town and may indicate that a wall was present already in the Early Dynastic period.[56]

Water and drainage works were not of such paramount importance in the North and the only evidence that we have is a finely constructed well from Level VI at T. Gawra, and an associated conduit.[57]

Let us now examine the house plans favoured in the North and see if it is possible to make any tentative deductions of a sociological nature from them. Unfortunately in both quantity and quality of material the North is far behind the South. At Mari a few houses of Early Dynastic date were excavated, but the area was small and the published plans inadequate. In the Agade period however we can say with certainty that the courtyard type of house was prevalent at least at Mari as in the South. One fine house plan was recovered from the so-called Maison-Rouge[58] at Mari. Some bronzes with the name of a son of Naram-Sin incised on them were found in the ruins of this house so its dating is reasonably secure. The basic plan of rooms round a central court remains unchanged. The kitchen is nearest the door and at the east end of it is a stair going up presumably to the roof as there is no mention of evidence for a second storey, and a paved "ablution area".

At T. Gawra however, what evidence there is suggests that the courtyard house was not present in Level VI of similar date. The evidence is difficult to assess because only the foundations of the houses were recovered so that the internal doorways and therefore the extent of each house cannot in most cases be distinguished. The houses seem to be smaller than their southern counterparts and perhaps both this and the lack of courtyards is to be attributed to the colder winter climate. It seems likely that what has been recovered are the remains of store and work rooms with the living rooms on the higher floors and undetected in the excavation. "Tower blocks" are well known in the Yemen today.

At T. Taya the protected area was larger than at Gawra, comprising as it did the citadel, the oval enclosure wall round part of the citadel, and the rectangular enclosure. Even so, some of the inhabited area lay outside the walls. Part of a house, S.W.6,[59] which was terraced on three levels, was excavated in the walled town, and another substantial building, W.1, was also explored. W.1 may well be something more than a private house judging from its size and the relative elaboration of its fittings which included a flight of stone steps and probably two bathrooms. Reade suggests that there may have been a shrine and a number of offices as well. The citadel also yielded remains of houses of this period including one substantial example with an arched door. The last house with which we have to deal is at least an unambiguous private house lying in the outer town of T. Taya and known as the S.1 house.[60] Again it is basically built round what is in this case a square courtyard with a lot of small rooms opening off it; the number of these rooms makes it a little unusual, but even more surprising is the discovery of a flight of steps leading down into a double cellar, the innermost part of which had the entrance to the family tomb in one wall. This tomb had been carved out of the bedrock and burial in it seems to have been restricted to adult male members of the household. The remains of three skeletons were found in it. Dr Reade, the excavator, also claims that there is evidence for the S.1 building having two storeys, which would agree with the evidence cited above for T. Gawra.

The evidence from T. Chuera is again confused; an area regarded originally by both Lauffray and Moortgat as "Artisan quarters" is now regarded by Moortgat as an elaborate mortuary chapel or chapels, on the grounds that what appear to be altars are found in several of the rooms which again are grouped round courtyards. There is no conclusive evidence in the South for shrines or chapels in private houses until the Ur III period, an exception being the shrine in house D at Khafaje; as this appears to have been a priest's house it cannot be used as evidence in dealing with private houses. Delougaz indicates one or two examples of what may have been shrines in the houses at Khafaje so that it is by no means impossible that the buildings at T. Chuera were houses, perhaps those of a priestly quarter. One unit, C., does appear to be larger and more elaborate than the others. The finds also seem to represent the ordinary contents of houses, and argue in favour of their having been domestic in character rather than mortuary.[61] The plan is that of a typical courtyard house, the only unusual feature being the long narrow entrance hall. The area lay below second millennium remains and the small finds indicate an Agade date for the upper levels; a deep sounding revealed more buildings at a considerably greater depth.

The practise of intramural burial does not seem to have been popular in the North, although earth graves were found in association with houses at T. Gawra in earlier levels. Tombs are also found, but always in association with the religious buildings. They are of mud-brick and stone, but only one is reported as having a corbelled roof; they mostly have matting, brick or even wooden covers and are orientated with the corners to the points of the compass as are the temples. There are also a few stone cists. The skeletal remains show a high percentage of infant and child burials which is the reverse of the situation in the South. Twenty-two tombs are found in Level VIIIC, only three in Level VIIIB and by Level VIIIA they have completely gone out of fashion, a development paralleled in the South.[62] The most interesting tomb in the North, if it can so be called, is the funerary complex[63] lying north-west of Steinbau I at T. Chuera; it consists of a range of five rooms set round two sides of a court of which four rooms form a unit apparently used for deposition of offerings; the fifth, which was a little isolated by a passage, contained the partially cremated bodies of two people, probably a man and woman, accompanied by at least two and possibly four young men armed with daggers and a spear. The internal fittings of the room with an arrangement of four short buttresses at right angles to one wall to form a series of three little "stalls" is slightly reminiscent of the hypogeum of 3rd Ur date at Tello.[64] This is the most elaborate grave known in North Syria, but its date is far from clear. There are certain parallels with Hittite burial customs known from texts, which Moortgat quoted, and which would point to a fairly late date, possibly around 2000, but if the Akkadian date suggested for Steinbau I can be substantiated then the proposed date of the tomb may have to be pushed back a little.

5*

Less elaborate tombs have been found at four other sites and belong to earlier periods in at least three of the cases. At Mari there are the three corbel vaulted stone built tombs[65] which lie beneath the floor of the Ishtar C temple. Only one contained any dateable grave goods, the other two having been completely robbed out. Tomb 300 contained pottery which the excavator describes as Scarlet Ware and various pottery and metal types, such as an axe of Woolley's A.13 type from Ur, were found. These all belong to the Early Dynastic period and taking into account the presence of the scarlet ware, to the early part of that period. At least one example of a grave of simpler type, stone walls, flat-roofed with slabs of stone, is also known from Mari.[66] The contents are not illustrated but the excavator dates this tomb too to the Early Dynastic period.

At Nineveh three long narrow vaults of unburnt brick were discovered,[67] the type of vault is not specified and from the photograph it is difficult to tell whether the true arch was employed or not. These vaults stood to a height of 15′ 6″ and one does question whether they were indeed graves at all. The finds associated with them were scattered, broken and uninformative; below floor level were Uruk Glockentopfe and the excavators suggest an Early Dynastic/Jemdet Nasr date for the construction itself. Finally Professor Mallowan in his survey of the Khabur mentions a "Mud-brick vaulted grave with domical roof" at T. Arbit[68] and states that the grave goods which included jewellery and weapons can be paralleled from the Royal Cemetery at Ur. It does seem then on the limited evidence available that the burial customs in the North, at least among a certain stratum of society, were broadly similar to those in the South though we have no evidence for human sacrifice in the Jazirah in the Early Dynastic period. The only evidence comes from T. Chuera where we have postulated a date at the end of the 3rd millennium.

Finally we have a small group of buildings which have previously been attributed to the Agade period but which appear now to be later. Dr Opificius has convincingly argued for Isin-Larsa and Old Babylonian dates respectively for temples G and F at Nuzi[69] which means that the town wall is now the only possibly Akkadian building from this site.

This concludes the survey of architectural remains from North Mesopotamia and North Syria and indicates that in general terms the architecture shows an overall similarity to that of the South, it used the same raw materials, had mastered the same techniques, and used some of the same basic plans. A later section will attempt to determine whether any closer parallels can be drawn between the two areas.

NOTES

[1] T.Braq. M.E.L.Mallowan, *Iraq* IX, p. 54; T.Hawa. S.Lloyd, *Iraq* V, p. 136; T.Jidle. M.E.L.Mallowan, *Iraq* VIII, p. 136.

[2] E.A.Speiser, *T. Gawra* I p. 36.

[3] *Syria* 1938, p. 4.

[4] Parrot, *MAM* III, p. 25.

[5] See Chapter I.

[6] M.E.L.Mallowan in *Iraq* IX, pl. VII.

[7] For the "Bent-axis temple", cf. A.Moortgat, *T. Chuera, 3rd campaign*, pl. 11 and p. 19.

[8] A.Parrot, *MAM*. III *passim*. For details of the decoration and internal layout of the Ninni-zaza temple, cf. pp. 23−25.

[9] W.Andrae, *Das Archaische Ishtar Tempel*. For the ivory figure, p. 56 and pl. 29.

[10] A.Parrot, *MAM*, I, p. 29−41.

[11] This complex which lay outside the town wall consists of a street or processional way lined with stele or standing stones, and a platform on which were found remains of a gatehouse and wall, and a megaron style temple with associated offering places. For details, A.Moortgat, *T. Chuera, 1st campaign*.

[12] A.Moortgat *T. Chuera, 3rd campaign*, plan. II.i. For the Troy Ia Megaron, Blegen, Caskey, Rawson and Sperling, *Troy* I, fig. 425. On the dating of megarons, cf. M.Mellink in *Comparative Chronologies*, ed. Ehrich and also J.Mellaart, *A.S.* IX, p. 131 and *C.A.H.* I, pt. 2, p. 374, and most recently, B.Hrouda, 'Die "Megaron" Bauten' in *Vorderasien. Anadolu* XIV, p. 1. Hrouda claims in this article that the earliest example of the Megaron plan can be seen in the Round House of Gawra XI A.

[13] For a brief English summary, cf. M.E.L.Mallowan in *Iraq* XXVIII, pt. I, p. 89 and A.Moortgat, *T. Chuera, 4th and 5th campaigns*.

[14] For the statuary, M.E.L.Mallowan, *op. cit.*, p. 92—93 and Moortgat, *op. cit. 4th campaign*, pp. 23—27. Abb. 16—20 and 21—24. Compare with Mesopotamian examples in Frankfort, H. Sculpture from the third millennium from T. Asmar and Khafaje.

[15] E.A.Speiser, *T. Gawra.* West temple, p. 26 and pl. XI. Eastern temple, p. 29 and pl. XI. For the typical tripartite plan of protoliterate Sumer, cf. White Temple at Warka or the Eridu VII temple. The porched tripartite plan can be traced back at Gawra itself to L.IX and possibly to L.X., A.L.Perkins, *Comparative archaeology of early Mesopotamia*, p. 174.

[16] S.Lloyd in *Iraq* VII, p. 15 and fig. 2.

[17] N.Egami, *T. eth Thalathat*, p. 7 and fig. 47; also M.E.L.Mallowan, *CAH.*, Vol. I, pt. i, Chapter VIII, p. 406.

[18] It has a large carefully plastered podium in the middle of the floor. For further details, E.A.Speiser, *T. Gawra* I, p. 29 and pl. XI.

[19] J.Reade, *Iraq* XXX, pt. 2, p. 241—242 and pl. LXXVIII.

[20] Reade, *op. cit.*, p. 253. Queen Pu-abi's diadem is a beautiful example of beadwork where hundreds of beads form the background for the small gold animals. C.L.Woolley, *Ur* II, pl. 140.

[21] A.Parrot, *Syria* XXI, fig. ID on plan.

[22] A.Parrot, *Syria* XXIX, p. 190—192 and *Syria* XXX, p. 216.

[23] A.Parrot, *Syria* XXXIX, p. 161—171 and *Syria* XLI, p. 5 and fig. I.

[24] For a reconstruction of this mosaic, cf. A.Parrot, *Syria* XXXIX, p. 164, fig. II.

[25] A.Parrot, *Syria* XXX, p. 200—204 and *Syria* XXXI, p. 159—166.

[26] A.Parrot in *Syria* XXI, p. 2, fig. IB and C on plan, B is Agade level; also fig. I4, p. 20 which illustrates a crude little wall painting of stick men and animals found in a room associated with the temple although it is not clear with which level of the temple Parrot associates it. Also *Syria* XXXI, p. 167—170.

[27] E.A.Speiser, *T. Gawra* I, p. 27 and pl. XI.

[28] For offering stands with triangular and sub-triangular openings, cf. P.Delougaz, *Pottery from the Diyala*, pl. 173.

[29] S.Lloyd, *Iraq* VII, p. 21 and figs. 3 and 4.

[30] A.Moortgat, *T. Chuera, Ist campaign.*

[31] J.Reade, T.Taya, *Iraq* XXX, pt. 2, p. 246 and 252—3.

[32] A.Parrot, *Syria* XLVII, p. 229.

[33] A.Parrot, *Syria* XXI, fig. IB and p. 2.

[34] A.Parrot, *Syria* XXI, fig. IA and pp. 8—14.

[35] W.Andrae, *Das Wiederstandene Assur*, p. 78.

[36] For Steinbau III, cf. A.Moortgat, *T. Chuera, 5th campaign*, pp. 4–8. For Steinbau I and II, *1st campaign*, pp. 22–25.

[37] A.Parrot in *Syria* '64, '65, '67, '69, '70 for the palace. N.B. in '64–67, PP1 is referred to as PP2 and PP2 as PP1; then the nomenclature is reversed.

[38] A.Parrot, *Syria* 1970, p. 231.

[39] E.A.Speiser, *T. Gawra* I, p. 30 and pl. XI; for the storage unit in L.VIIIB, p. 31 and pl. X.

[40] E.A.Speiser, *op. cit.*, p. 35, pl. IX.

[41] Speiser, *op. cit.*, p. 36 and pl. IX.

[42] C.Preusser, *Die Wohnhäuser von Assur*, p. 5–7 and pls. I, 2.

[43] M.E.L.Mallowan in *Iraq* IX, p. 64, section by Guildford Bell and pl. LX.

[44] *Ibid.* pl. LXIIA and pp. 72–73.

[45] *Ibid.*, p. 71.

[46] M.E.L.Mallowan in *Iraq* III, p. 15.

[47] A.Parrot, *MAM* I, p. 48–49 and *Syria* XVII, p. 12–13 and plan.

[48] A.Moortgat, *T. Chuera, 2nd campaign plan*.

[49] This may prove an erroneous impression as more towns are completely excavated. The Akkadian level at T. Gawra is planned round a small open square, cf. also K.Polanyi, 'Marketless trading in Hammurabi's time' in *Trade and market in the early empires* for an interesting though not wholly convincing discussion.

[50] E.A.Speiser, *T. Gawra* I. Gawra VI is discussed on pp. 19–21.

[51] A.Moortgat, *T. Chuera, 3rd campaign*, plans II and III.

[52] Speiser, *op. cit.*, pp. 19–21 and pl. VII.

[53] J.Reade, *Iraq* XXX, pt. 2, pp. 241–243 for citadel and *Iraq* XXXIII, pt. 2, pp. 92–94 for town wall.

[54] J.Reade, *Iraq* XXX, pt. 2, p. 252, for the gate-house, pp. 246–248. For Nuzi, R.Starr, *Nuzi* I, p. 325–328; for T. Chuera, cf. note 47 this chapter; for T. Jidle, M.E.L.Mallowan in *Iraq* VIII, p. 118; for T. Khoshi, S.Lloyd in *Iraq* VII, p. 20.

[55] Cf. aerial photographs in the preliminary survey carried out by Lauffray and pub. in *Ann. Arch. Syriennes*, Vol. 4, 1954, p. 140. Also *T. Chuera, 1st campaign*.

[56] W.Andrae, *Das Wiederstandene Assur*, p. 62.

[57] Speiser, *op. cit.*, p. 32 and pl. X.

[58] A.Parrot, *Syria* XXXII, p. 194–199.

[59] J.Reade, *Iraq* XXXIII, pt. 2, Houses S.W.6 and W.1, pp. 94–95. Arched door in house on citadel, *Iraq* XXX, pt. 2, p. 252.

[60] J.Reade, *Iraq* XXXIII, pt. 2, p. 96—98 and fig. 3.

[61] For a description of the Artisan quarter, A.Moortgat, *T. Chuera, 1st campaign*, pp. 33—39 and 2nd, p. 1—11. For possible shrines in private houses in the Early Dynastic period, cf. Delougaz, *P.H.D.*, pp. 11—12 and p. 151.

[62] For the Gawra tombs, cf. A.Tobler, *T. Gawra* II. For dating, Table A, p. 54 and Table D, p. 68. The tomb with the corbelled roof is attributed to L.XI and is described on p. 72. The tomb no. is G.36.120. The high proportion of child burials is discussed on p. 78.

[63] A.Moortgat, *T. Chuera, 1st campaign*, p. 26—32, *3rd campaign*, p. 29—40 and plan III.

[64] A.Parrot, *Revue d'Ass.* XXIX, no. 2, p. 45 and for a different interpretation of the Hypogeum, one now more widely accepted, M-T.Barrelet, *Iraq* XVII, pt. 2, p. 100.

[65] A.Parrot, *Syria* 1938 p. 4; 1937, p. 60; also *MAM* I, p. 11.

[66] A.Parrot, *Syria* 1935, p. 9 and pl. II.4

[67] *L.A.A.A.* Vol. XIX, p. 78.

[68] M.E.L.Mallowan, *Iraq* IV, p. 127.

[69] R.Starr, *Nuzi* I, pp. 64—72 and plans 6 and 7. For redating, R.Opificius, *Terracottareliefen*, p. 16.

CHAPTER IV

Architectural evidence from representational art and in the texts

Our evidence comes from three main types of material; the most numerous examples are provided by seals and seal impressions; as the glyptic repertoire becomes more stereotyped towards the end of the third millennium they are of less value. The second group is provided by representations on stone vases and troughs, notably on the steatite vases which are found from Mari in the West to Mohenjo-Daro in the East; and the third, numerically small but unusually interesting is provided by actual models of houses and temples. Lastly, we have a few miscellaneous fragments of evidence such as house plans drawn on clay tablets, of which four examples are known for the Akkadian period, decoration on painted pottery, and fragments of inlay like those from the temple frieze at Al Ubaid. No new facts emerge from the examination of this evidence, but one or two tentative suggestions made by excavators can be corroborated, and some idea of temporary structures leaving little trace in the archaeological record can be obtained.

An analysis of the semi-pictorial signs appearing on material from SIS IV at Ur led Legrain to identify two "architectural" signs, the first showing a rectilinear door or facade, usually associated with scenes of libation and ritual, and the second a round topped door or facade which is almost always associated with scenes of husbandry.[1] It seems permissible to identify the first group of buildings as temples, particularly as the facade is often associated with the Inanna symbol and other "standards"; it would seem that sometimes the door was used to symbolise the whole building. Such buildings appear on seals and seal impressions from the Uruk period onwards. Examples can be found which depict stift-mosaic in place on the temple walls, triangular windows, sometimes employed alongside square ones, in the same building. On one or possibly two early seals (respectively from

Susa and Khafaje) there is some indication of clerestory lighting over the central area of the building which in a temple of classic tripartite plan, presumably housed the shrine.[2] The recent finds at Uruk which indicate that the vertical section of Temple C had indeed been roofed[3] are a further argument in favour of some form of clerestory lighting as the shrine would have been intolerably dim without it. A protoliterate seal from Susa actually shows small square windows in the raised central portion of the roof.

In one or two seals the beams on which the flat roof of the building is laid are shown projecting end-on over the façade;[4] a pitched roof is never shown. Another seal from Susa[5] shows a magnificent building, presumably a temple, as the whole building appears to be sprouting three pairs of horns, the symbol of divinity. The building stands on an elaborately niched and recessed plinth or platform such as is known from excavations on the ziggurat at Eridu.

Turning now to the round-topped sign, it seems to represent a type of reed byre which is commonly depicted on seals. Basically these byres appear to be hemispherical, the roof often being decorated with what appears to be the reed equivalent of corn dollies. The byres look to be constructed on the same principle as the reed houses made today by the Marsh Arabs of Southern Iraq. A frame is made consisting of a line of arches formed by bending down and lashing together bundles of reeds, the walls being made by hanging reed mats between the reed "ribs" of the house. Some of the decorative addenda mentioned above as occurring on the roofs of the byres may result from the method of lashing together two bundles of reeds at the apex of the arches forming the "ribs" of the building.[7] Other decorations protruding from the roof, however, appear to be the standards mentioned above as occurring on temple façades. The so-called Inanna symbol is one of the commonest as is a pole with loops on either side and a curious triangular object on the end of a pole somewhat like the "hoe" later associated with Martu. It is possible that these standards do not mark the innate sacredness of the herd of the building, but rather brand them as belonging to the god whose standard they bear. Delougaz has suggested[8] that one type of standard is always found with sheep and another with cattle, but this distinction does not hold good on further scrutiny. The Inanna symbol is usually associated with sheep, but on two seals from Ur is found with cattle.[9] The ringed pole is usually found with cattle, but can occur with sheep.

Other architectural representations are less informative, for instance seals of the Agade period often show the gates of heaven being opened to allow the sun to start his journey, or the bull of heaven to rampage. These gates are of little use for our purpose as they are divorced from any sort of building or enclosure. The representations of a god, often Ea, within his shrine are equally unhelpful, as the shrine is usually portrayed schematically as a rectangular box, although on one seal from Ur the roof beams again seem to be shown.[10] The final class of architecturally informative seals shows what Amiet is convinced is the building of a ziggurat; the structure is of several types, one shows a humped structure with a rounded top, the second tent-shaped objects, and the third staged structures. The humped object looks like nothing so much as a haycock, the second in at least one example appears to be a frame for drying fish or possibly smoking it. The third however can hardly be interpreted other than as a ziggurat.[11] One fine example from Kish illustrated by Amiet has four super-imposed stages each decorated with recesses or niches. Two seals from the treasure found in the Early Dynastic palace at Mari show ziggurats, one of two stages and one of three stages.[12] These seals were found in the cache of treasure which also contained a bead inscribed with the name of Mes-anne-padda. This would agree with the archaeological evidence which also suggests that staged ziggurats were found in Mesopotamia by Early Dynastic III.[13] One or two other seals are known from Susa which also seem to show men building a structure on top of a platform, but the platform is not stepped and the structure is dome-shaped. It looks more like a kiln, or oven, than a religious building; it should perhaps be compared to the circular structures on raised bases found at Khafaje and in the P.C.B. building at Kish; both Delougaz and Moorey suggest that these objects had some important practical function to fulfil.[14]

Two seals from Mesopotamia and one purchased in Luxor show

multiple doorways with curious bowed-down lintels which provide a link with the next class of evidence, that provided by decorated stone vessels.[15] The biggest category is that of the steatite vases and their clay imitations, which apparently show facades of buildings having multiple doors and windows with characteristically sagging lintels. Delougaz in his interesting article on these pots has suggested that this type of lintel was used as a "spacer" to keep the uprights of the doorframe apart, the pressure from the uprights having the effect of causing the lintel to bulge downwards.[16] The walls of these buildings are often shown as ornamented with zig-zag and other patterns which in the past have been thought to represent the designs woven into the reed mats of which the walls were constructed. However, it now appears that contrary to the opinion expressed by Mr Durrani in his comprehensive article on these vessels, they were not native to Mesopotamia, but may have been made in South Iran.[17] The main bulk of examples from T. Yahya, not all of which have architectural motifs, are found in Level IVB and are dated by their excavator to 3000–2500 B.C. which would seem to place them earlier than the majority of the Mesopotamian examples; the earliest of these come from Early Dynastic II horizons at Khafaje.[18] There is also evidence at T. Yahya for the local production and manufacture of these pots. Reed architecture is not native to these Iranian regions and therefore unless the people of T. Yahya were catering specifically for the Mesopotamian market by reproducing Mesopotamian reed mudhifs on these vessels, the likelihood is either that the architectural pots originate elsewhere, possibly in the Gulf where reed houses are found, or that the patterns on the walls reflect fashions in building to be found at and around T. Yahya itself, that is to say, building in mud-brick or perhaps stone rather than reed. The purpose of these pots is also in doubt; it has been suggested that they held cosmetic pastes or similar unguents. This explanation fits the vessels from Baluchistan and India which are compartmented and in the case of the example from Mohenjo-Daro have lids.[19] However, none of the Mesopotamian examples has a lid and many of them have been found in religious contexts; a number of fragments were found in the Ninnizaza temple and in Cella 18 of the Ishtar A temple at

Mari, and two in the Sin temple at Khafaje. One of the non-architectural examples from Ur came from the tomb of Pu-abi and a second from another grave in the Royal Cemetery, both of which could reasonably be regarded as non-secular contexts.[20] The majority of the rest of the finds are unstratified. On present evidence we can say with Delougaz that they had some ritual significance, though this is in effect an admission that their purpose is unknown.

The presence of these pots in the Royal Cemetery at Ur establishes their presence in Early Dynastic III, but none have yet been found in Akkadian contexts. However, the examples from Bampur and the surrounding area are dated by Miss de Cardi to c.1900.[21] As they are made in grey pottery, apparently imitating the steatite examples, it is reasonable to postulate that the Bampur pots are the last debased examples of a tradition which seems to cover much of the third millennium. As we have seen, the T. Yahya examples may go back to the beginning of the third millennium, the ones from Khafaje are in an Early Dynastic II context; the ones from Ur in Early Dynastic III levels; the examples from Ishtar A Temple at Mari in late Early Dynastic III, and the pottery copies from Bampur may be as late as 2000–1900. We must also reconsider the theory dealing with their supposed Mesopotamian origins. The discovery of a workshop at T. Yahya and a mine in the vicinity coupled with the early date for this site make the Southern Iranian origin of some types almost certain. The wide dispersal of these vessels in time and space is an interesting example of the mobility of goods in the third millennium. The recent finds of many fragments of steatite vases on Persian Gulf sites may perhaps indicate that these vessels travelled by a sea as well as a land route from Iran to Mesopotamia. It is also possible that some vases were manufactured in Arabia where steatite is also found.

Buildings of other sorts also appear on other stone vessels, known from the excavations at several sites. A fine example showing a reed byre, paralleled exactly on the seals, came from the Small Temple at Khafaje, while another, probably of Jemdet Nasr date, comes from T. al'Ubaid and also seems to depict a byre built on a framework of reeds.[23] A limestone stele dated by Moortgat to Early Dynastic II is particularly interesting as it shows a king or priest accompanied by a woman, making offering before a tall thin building which is possibly a temple, but more probably an altar of the type found by Andrae in the Ishtar temple at Assur.[24] It seems to have the same stepped top as the models from Assur, a type also represented on seals, sometimes with offerings depicted actually in position on them. Another early Early Dynastic example comes from Ur where a stone plaque shows a man pouring a libation in front of a doorway which has the standards one on either side and also the sagging lintel which occurs on the steatite vases, only here its bow is upwards instead of downwards.[25] It seems likely however that the constructional principle involved was the same. Finally the milking frieze which decorated the temple facade at Al Ubaid also shows cattle emerging from a byre with the lintel this time drooping down again.[26] The frequency with which this device is portrayed suggests that it was a technique commonly used in the third millennium.

The evidence from the small group of pottery models of "houses" is ambiguous and difficult to interpret. By chance, most of the evidence comes from the north of Mesopotamia, from Mari, Nuzi and Assur and may to some extent reflect local fashions. One model was recently found during the American survey of the Warka region as a surface find. Two model houses were discovered at Mari, during excavations in the town area. Both appeared to have been carefully deposited, one under the road and the other, which had been disturbed and broken, in and around the Red House of the Akkadian town.[27] They are identical, according to the excavator, and both represent circular buildings with a square room or court with a hearth in the centre. The central "room" is linked to the outer wall by a number of cross walls which form several small compartments. The first problem is to decide whether these models represent a small, square building surrounded by a yard and a circular wall, or on the other hand a circular building with a square courtyard in the centre. The presence of four small horizontal loops in the corners of the square enclosure suggest that it may have had a lid, possibly symbolising a roof; these models seem to represent the first type of structure for which there is no archaeological parallel in

Mesopotamia. The only circular structures we have archaeological evidence for in Mesopotamia belong to an earlier period; at T. Gawra in the Uruk period and at Halaf, even earlier, circular structures are found divided internally into rooms and are believed to be fortified houses. The Round House in Level XIA at T. Gawra may even possibly have had an open court in the centre. It is these buildings which our model houses most closely resemble. Circular buildings which resemble our model and which date to EBA I were found at Yanik Tepe in Azerbaijan. The excavator describes Circle 1, which most closely resembles our model, as a granary. One of the rooms in the complete model from Mari has an oven in it and there seems to be no reason to regard the model as anything other than a house. We have no evidence for circular religious architecture by the third millenium. So far the only concrete evidence for circular buildings comes from the North so we may perhaps hazard the guess that this type of dwelling was not used in the South. Even when we accept the Mari models as being houses we cannot explain the thinking which led to their burial, filled with pots, in positions which must have had some special, possibly prophylactic significance. The find of an offering stand at Nuzi shaped like a circular tower is perhaps relevant in this context.[28] This unstratified example has triangular windows and an arched door. Unfortunately neither of these features can be paralleled on the Mari models. Possibly they were features of religious architecture. Other offering stands from Nuzi and more recently from T. Chuera appear to show rectilinear tower-like buildings sometimes several storeys high.[29] Once again such a feature has not been recognised in excavation, but this does not mean that it did not exist. The builders certainly had the technical competence to build "tower blocks" if they had wanted to.

The model found on a site WS 387 North-East of Uruk is an extremely interesting one in that it appears to have close parallels with an excavated example, the earliest Jemdet Nasr Inanna Temple at Nippur. The model was found associated with pottery "not later than Early Dynastic I" which also agrees with the proposed comparison. The model shows a bipartite shrine of our type C with a courtyard in front of it. There is a cella and ante-cella and both are roofed, though the presence of a large skylight in the roof of the cella may possibly explain why the excavators of the Inanna Temple considered that the cella there had not been roofed at all.[30] From Khafaje we have the so-called cult wagon from Sin Temple VIII which has been heavily restored;[31] the house it depicts may have been modified to support the little pots it carries. It shows the usual flat roof with beam ends projecting, forming perches for doves nestling under the roof. A ladder leans against the wall presumably for access to the roof although internal stairs are known, certainly by the Agade period. The zig-zag pattern on the end wall, which might be taken to represent the characteristic herring-bone method of laying bricks is in fact a restoration. A final example from the South comes from the cemetery at Ubaid and may therefore be earlier than our period. It represents part of a house with a pitched roof and so is almost certainly imported, perhaps from Iran.

Some of the best known model "houses" were found at Assur where Andrae discovered a group of them, still in position, in the cella of the Ishtar H and G temples, where they seem to have served as dumb-waiters for offerings or perhaps as subsidiary altars.[32] Similar objects are known on plaques and seals where they are often shown with offerings of food and drink actually in position. The altars represent two parallel, rectangular rooms lying side by side and lit with rectangular and triangular windows which on House I occur together. Both rooms are flat-roofed, but one is lit by clerestory windows above the level of the flat roof of the second room. Thie gives a stepped profile and two flat surfaces, the roofs, on which vessels or containers could be placed. A curious feature of the "houses" is that several of them are decorated with animals in relief on the facades; one has birds under the roof and snakes climbing the walls, another has birds alone and a third two animals identified as lions perched on the roof.[33] Possibly each of these models was dedicated to a different god who could be identified to the worshipper by the animal depicted on the altar, in the same way that Catholic saints may often be identified by their symbols. The question now arises as to whether these models represent actual shrines, actual altars or merely the general concept of a shrine or an altar. They bear little relation to the altars known from excavation though these are sometimes stepped and have been found with architectural decoration on their frontals. One of the most notable examples is of course the altar in the main Jemdet Nasr level of the Eye temple at T. Braq.[34] There is no provision on these models for the pouring of liquid offerings, a common feature in excavated examples. On the other hand no excavated shrine has yielded a ground plan which when reconstructed would resemble these models. However in some cases in the House temples of our type D the sanctuary and an adjacent room do lie side by side and parallel to one side of the central court. The Ishtar temple itself falls into this category, but the arrangement of the rooms is a little asymmetric. A better parallel is provided by Sin Temples VI—IX at Khafaje[35] where the cella and service rooms lie adjacent to each other and parallel to the west side of the courtyard. Such a unit could be reconstructed to resemble the model "houses" from Assur. They might alternatively be reconstructed like our bipartite temples of group C. It is possible then that these models are intended to represent the actual sanctuary of a House Plan temple or a Bipartite shrine, but perhaps it is more realistic to interpret them as a generalised representation of a temple, possibly adapted to fit their particular function as altars. Certainly in general terms there is nothing incompatible with their being models of part, or whole, of a shrine. On the other hand it is possible to say with a fair degree of certainty that they bear little resemblance to the altars known from excavation and none at all to the most typical secular house plans.

Next we come to a little doodle thought to represent a hut, painted on a sherd from Jemdet Nasr,[36] which if accurate appears to depict our one and only chimney. (Upside down the hut becomes a convincing boat with a large rudder!) Two tablets from T. Asmar have been found which interestingly depict what are presumed to be architects' plans for houses.[37] Unfortunately for us a plan alone is given but no elevation. Each of the tablets, both of which are thought to be Akkadian in date, depict the classic "fully flanked" courtyard plan which as we have seen, often had to be drastically modified in real life to fit into the available space. A partially destroyed plan on a tablet from Nippur shows a courtyard with rooms on three sides and what appears to be a second subsidiary court. A stair is also shown in the "hall".

Another example, thought to come from Tello and to be Agade in date, again partially destroyed, is illustrated by Thureau-Daugin in his "Recueil de Tablettes Chaldéennes" and is interpreted by Lenzen as depicting a temple. It does bear some resemblance to the design of the Enlil Temple at Nippur, but it is not impossible that it represents a private house. It is unique in that the dimensions of each room are listed; the room called "pa-pah" translated by Lenzen as "cella" might be the domestic chapel. Two fragmentary plans from Tello show respectively the corner of an enclosure wall and the plan of a (?)temple enceinte showing the general layout of offices such as cowsheds and weaving shed.

As we warned at the beginning of this section, nothing new has emerged from a study of architectural representations in the art of the third millennium, but certain features which were deduced from the excavated buildings can be confirmed. For instance, the fact that we have only one representation of a pitched roof on any type of building is striking. A flat roof of course uses less timber than a pitched one, an important consideration in the South where no hard timber was available locally, and the roof area provided extra living space in densely populated areas such as we find in some of the tell towns. The roof was also used in the temples for ritual purposes. On the other hand a flat roof needed a good deal more in the way of upkeep. The question of lighting has also been clarified; good evidence has been found for clerestory lighting and both triangular and rectangular windows are attested. The problem of the roofing of the central court or room in many of the smaller private houses has not been clarified by our study which has provided no further evidence on this particular point. The most controversial suggestion is based on the circular house models from Mari and on the strength of these it is tentatively suggested that circular houses may have continued in use in the North after their last proved appearance in Gawra XIA and that these circular buildings may also have been built with an open court in the centre. There is no evidence to suggest their occurrence in the South. We have also seen that there is ample representational evidence for the type of light structure which would leave little trace in the archaeological record. Houses, byres and sheepfolds were made of reeds probably by the same techniques which are used by the Marsh Arabs of the Shatt al Arab today; houses may well have been constructed of them until quite a late period. When warning Utnapistim of the approaching flood Ea addresses his house with the words "Reed hut, reed hut, wall, wall. Reed hut hearken, . . .".[38] We cannot use this as documentary evidence for the existence of reed houses in the third millennium, it may well represent a conscious archaism on the part of the author, but it is an interesting confirmation of a usage for which only slight evidence has been found in the archaeological record. There is in fact sadly little additional evidence to be obtained from the texts. Passing references to buildings occur in various epics as well as in the inscriptions of the rulers themselves, but they are usually so wrapped in rhetoric as to tell us little more than that the building was constructed. In the VIth tablet of the Creation epic, there is an interesting mention of the use of brick moulds by the Annunaki to fashion the bricks out of which E-Sagila was built,[39] but of the form of the building little is told us except that it was a stage-tower.

Two slightly more informative references are known to the building of Uruk, and in particular to its city wall. Gilgames is first credited with having founded the double wall which encircled the city, and he built it of burnt brick.[40] This was a source of pride to the builder as obviously the labour and expense of providing burnt brick was considerably greater than that needed to supply sun-dried bricks. Even in the Ur III period burnt brick was usually reserved for the outer skin of brickwork, as indeed may have been the case with the walls of Uruk. The poem also refers to the outer wall as having "a brightness like that of copper" which is difficult to understand unless it is an anachronistic reference to the brilliantly glazed walls and gates of the Neo-Babylonian period. In the Lugalbanda epic Enmerkar is credited with the founding of Uruk where he is said to have built for fifty years and the walls are said to have stretched across the plain like the nets for catching birds.[41] It is plain from other references in the Gilgames epic that the city walls protected orchards and gardens as well as residential and business quarters.[42] The religious compound was often, as at Uruk, protected by an inner wall of its own.

An interesting text of the Larsa period copies a description supposedly found in an inscription of Naram-Sin of a walled city, apparently in North Syria where just such a multiple walling is described although it is not specifically stated that the innermost wall is that of the temple area.[43] The same situation may also be reflected in the plan at T. Gawra where in Level VI one wall was found on the crown of the tell, surrounding the citadel, and a second was traced some way down the flank of the mound. It is by no means impossible that a third ring of fortification existed at plain level. T. Taya, too, has three different fortification walls.

NOTES

[1]   L.Legrain, *Ur* III. Archaic seal impressions, pl. 40 and P.Delougaz. 'Animals emerging from a hut', in *J.N.E.S.*, 27, p. 184 ff.

[2]   For windows, H.Frankfort, *S.F.D.*, pl. 5, no. 34; for clerestory lighting and stift-mosaic, P.Amiet, *G.M.A.*, pl. A, no. 5, pl. 16, no. 272.

[3]   H.Lenzen, in *Archaeology* 17, p. 122.

[4]   H.Frankfort, *S.F.D.*, pl. 5, no. 30 and pl. 77, no. 836.

[5]   P.Amiet, *G.M.A.*, pl. A, no. 3 and pl. 46, no. 659, also L.LeBreton in *Iraq* XIX, pl. XXIV and p. 115.

[6]   L.Legrain, *Ur* III, pl. 40.

[7]   For the construction of these huts, cf. W.Thesiger, *The Marsh Arabs*, pl. 87, 88 and 90.

[8]   P.Delougaz in *J.N.E.S.*, 27, p. 196.

[9]   For cattle shown with the Inanna symbol, cf. Legrain, *Ur* III, no. 337 and 342.

[10]   C.L.Woolley, *Ur* II, pl. 215, no. 364.

[11]   P.Amiet, *G.M.A.*, p. 181 ff. For type 1) pl. 109, no. 1443
                                    2) pl. 109, esp. no. 1448
                                    3) pl. 109, no. 1444

[12]   For the example from Kish, Amiet, *op. cit.*, pl. 109, no. 1444; for the Mari seals, A.Parrot, *M.A.M.* IV, no. 4445 on pl. XIX and no. 4451, pl. XX.

[13]   Cf. Chapter II.

[14]   For the seals, cf. Amiet, *op. cit.*, pl. 16, nos. 267, 268 and 269; also P.R.S.Moorey in *Iraq* XXVI, pt. 2. The plano-convex building at Kish, p. 88.

[15] For these seals, Briggs Buchanan, *Catalogue of Ancient Near Eastern seals in the Ashmolean Museum*, no. 1057, on pl. 64 and p. 211, seal from Luxor. Also E.Porada, *Seals*, pl. XVII, no. 108E (E.D. III) and Woolley, *Ur* II, pl. 200, no. 107(E.D. III) of lapis-lazuli from P.G. 55. If the date attributed to the Ashmolean seal (peripheral Jemdet Nasr) is correct, then it is especially interesting as it becomes one of the earliest examples of this type of doorway depicted outside T. Yahya and suggests a direct link between Iran and Egypt in the early third millennium, a possibility also suggested by recent finds on the West coast of the Persian Gulf.

[16] P.Delougaz, 'Architectural representations on steatite vases', in *Iraq* XXII, pp. 91—93.

[17] F.A.Durrani in *Ancient Pakistan* I. Stone vases as evidence of connection between Mesopotamia and the Indus valley, p. 96. Also C.C.Lamberg-Karlovsky, *Excavations at T. Yahya*. Iran 1967—1969, esp. p. 61. Cf. also *Iran* IX—X for interim reports. A piece of a steatite plaque shown on pl. 11a in *Iran* X closely resembles the pot from Adab with its stepped "ziggurat" motif. This motif is now known to occur in Afghanistan, Seistan and South Turkmenia, at Mundigak, Shahr-i-Sokhta and Namazga respectively. The example from Adab is unstratified and that from Yahya is thought to be from L.IVa.

[18] Delougaz, *op. cit.*, p. 94.

[19] Durrani, *op. cit.*, p. 92.

[20] A.Parrot, *M.A.M.* III, p. 180 and pl. LXXI, p. 182, fig. 228; also *MAM* I, pl. XLVI, XLVII and L, p. 113—115 and p. 119. Woolley, *Ur* II, pl. CLXXVIII and an untraced pot illustrated in *Ur* IV, pl. XXXV, no. U. 18865.

[21] B.de Cardi, *Excavations at Bampur*, p. 268—269 and in the same volume, E.C.L.During-Caspers on the carved stone and incised greyware, p. 319 ff. Lamberg-Karlovsky in his article, 'Trade mechanisms in Indus-Mesopotamian inter-relations' in *J.A.O.S.* 92.i would update the Bampur sequence and equate Yahya IVb (early/mid third mill.) with the end of the Bampur sequence, *i.e.* Bampur VI.

[22] G.Burkholder in *Artibus Asiae* XXXIII, pt. 4, p. 306—322 for a catalogue of steatite fragments from the Persian Gulf. E.C.L.During-Caspers in *East and West*, Vol. 21, 1-2, p.30, for the presence of steatite in Arabia.

[23] P.Delougaz, *P.S.T.* p. 104, fig. 93. Also A.Moortgat, *Art of Mesopotamia*, pl. 17.

[24] A.Moortgat, *op. cit.*, pls. 31—34 and p. 26. For the Assur model altars, cf. this chapter, p. 72.

[25] Woolley, *Ur* IV, pl. 39. U. 6831 and p. 45.

[26] Hall and Woolley, *Al Ubaid*, pl. XXXI 1—3 and Delougaz in *J.N.E.S.*, 27, p. 191 and fig. 15.

27 A.Parrot, *M.A.M.* III, p. 295, fig. 312 and pl. LXXXII for complete model and p. 305 and pl. LXXXIV for broken one.

28 R.Starr, *Nuzi*, pl. 114e. A circular incense burner apparently depicting a building with an upper storey comes from stratum XIII at T. Gawra and a similar example from L.XI, cf. A.Tober, *T. Gawra*, II, pl. LXXVIIId and pl. CXLVIII, no. 435.

29 R.Starr, *Nuzi* pl. 61 a and b. For examples from T. Chuera, cf. A.Moortgat, *1st campaign*, Abb. 25, p. 28 and *3rd campaign*, Abb. 22, p. 29.

30 Adams and Nissen, *The Uruk countryside*, p. 215, fig. 83. For the Inanna temple, cf. Chap. I above.

31 P.Delougaz, *P.F.D.*, p. 86 and pls. 82–83.

32 W.Andrae, *Die archaischen Ishtar Tempel*, pp. 36–37, Abb. 5 and tafs. 14–16.

33 *Tonhaus* I (taf. 14 in Andrae *op. cit.*) has birds and snakes, No. 2 has birds only and II and III have lions. (taf. 15a–b).

34 M.E.L.Mallowan. T.Braq in *Iraq* IX, p. 32, pls. II–IV.

35 Delougaz, *P.S.T.*, pl. XII.

36 E.Mackay, *Jemdet Nasr*, pl. LXXX.

37 Plans from T. Asmar are illustrated in Delougaz, *P.H.D.*, pl. 65, and the Nippur example in McCown and Haines, *Nippur* I, pl. 52 a and b; the example from Tello in Thureau-Dangin, *Receuil de tablettes Chaldéenes*, p. 66, no. 145, 147 and 148. For a complete list, cf. *Reallexicon der Assyriologie*, Band 3.9., p. 666–667.

38 There are many translations available. For a "classic" version, cf. J.B.Pritchard, *The Ancient Near East in texts and pictures*, p. 66 and for a more modern prose version, N.K.Sandars, *The epic of Gilgames*, p. 105.

39 A.Heidel, *The Babylonian Genesis*, Tablet VI, 62–63 and for the brick moulds, line 36 on p. 63.

40 A.Heidel, *op. cit.*, tablet I, lines 9–12 and line 18, also Tablet XI, 21–22.

41 C.Wilcke, *Das Lugalbanda epos* , line 297–305.

42 A.Heidel, *op. cit.*, Tablet XI, lines 305–307.

43 F.R.Kraus, 'Ein altakkadisches Festungsbild' in *Iraq* X, p. 81; also G.Gadd and L.Legrain, *Ur* Texts I, no. 275.

CHAPTER V

Having examined the evidence from both North and South it is important to, in the classic phrase, compare and contrast the results in an attempt to assess among other things the stage of technological, social and economic development reached in each area; the amount of interaction between the two areas and the importance of foreign influence, foreign that is to both regions. Various obvious comparisons can be made at once. The evidence from both areas is archaeologically sub-standard and there is a heavy imbalance in favour of monumental architecture. A representative spectrum of sites, from small village through to city, is not available from either area although a somewhat wider range is found in the South. Surveys conducted by Professor Adams, Dr Nissen, Dr Wright and others in the South indicate the presence of a stratified hierarchy of settlement sites by the Early Dynastic period in which typically a large centre such as Uruk, was surrounded by a belt of intensively cultivated land up to a radius of 15 km, which provided the basic foodstuffs for its citizens. Outside this belt it seems that a normal hierarchy of town/village/ hamlet could be identified, although the spatial distribution of sites was always largely determined by the courses of canals and rivers and the problem of wind erosion and deposition has undoubtedly blurred and possibly distorted the results. The importance of the waterways militated against the establishment of the classic honeycomb pattern of settlement as expounded by Christaller, Haggett and others. It is very desirable that similar surveys should be attempted in the North, it has indeed been argued in the past that the larger towns and cities did not exist in the North; however, the recent excavations at T. Taya indicate that this site covers an area equal to that of many Southern sites and it is to be expected that further surveys will bring to light other urban centres.

The techniques and building materials in each area are broadly comparable, with certain localised differences. The plano-convex brick is found only rarely in the North and only one example of brick laid in the herringbone pattern so typical of the South is reported in the North, and that in a pre-Early Dynastic context.[1] Reed architecture is unlikely to occur far north of the natural habitat of the reed, and it seems that wood and stone were more widely used in the North where they were more freely available; indeed wooden structures may have replaced the reed ones of the South as byres and other temporary buildings though we have no direct evidence of this. The only evidence we have for buildings of two or more storeys also comes from the North and perhaps reflects the wider use of wooden flooring and roofing timbers. Evidence for a second storey is claimed for a house at T. Taya and several of the offering stands from Nuzi show two or sometimes three floors.[2] It is possible from the evidence of the pottery models that the whole superstructure was of wood. Stone is also more widely used in the North, once more for the practical reason that it was more immediately available. It occurs in footings and foundations, in tombs and cists and at T. Chuera is used prodigally in the construction of the Steinbaus. We have already shown that both areas had a working knowledge of all the basic architectural forms and by the Agade period had become precise in their construction. Technologically then, both areas had reached approximately the same level of competence although there was probably a higher level of artistic sophistication in the South, judging from architectural decorations such as the ornamentation on the temple facade at Al Ubaid.

If we begin our detailed comparison by a study of the religious architecture two features are immediately apparent, two types found in the South do not occur in the North. Our type C, the Bipartite temple with a broad cella as represented at Nippur by the earliest Inanna temple, and by the model found on the surface of a mound by the Warka survey team, does not occur in the North. Moortgat has claimed that the broad cella seen in type C was a peculiarly Neo-Sumerian feature as exemplified in the Ningal Temple in the Gigparku at Ur, and the Enki Temple of Amar-Sin, also at Ur.[3] However, as we have shown, a shrine of very similar proportions was found at Nippur, and was attributed by the excavators to the Jemdet Nasr period. The existence of such a plan in the Jemdet Nasr and the occurrence of a similar temple model as a surface find in what seems likely to be a Jemdet Nasr/Early Dynastic I context raises the problem of the apparent gap in time between these early examples and the Ur III instances quoted above. In view of the incomplete nature of the evidence it is not unreasonable to suggest that the plan continued in use throughout the third millennium, and to hope that further excavation will confirm this. The plan may grow in popularity in the Ur III period, but the concept is a long established one.

The Temple Oval, our type E, does not occur in the North either and appears on present evidence to be a fairly short-lived conceit even in the South. On present evidence there is nothing to show that any of the Mesopotamian Ovals survived long into the Akkadian period. The exception is the Barbar temple in Bahrein which apparently continued to flourish into the second millennium.

To balance the absence of these two types, the North has produced a further two types not present in the South, of which Type G, the Megaron temple, is particularly interesting on account of its obvious affinities with the early architecture of Anatolia and Greece. A certain amount of agreement now exists on the definition of the term "Megaron"; in the simplest form it is applied to a rectangular building whose side walls are extended to form a porch in front of the building. A stricter definition of the term requires that the structure have the internal fittings typical of the classical examples, such as a raised hearth, sleeping platforms and a pillared porch. Even if the first and more generalised definition is used it is difficult to accept Hrouda's suggestion that the central portion of the Round House at T. Gawra is the earliest known example of the megaron. The more widely held view that Troy I and now the EBA level XVII at Beycesultan have produced the earliest megara outside Greece, still carries more weight. Lloyd makes a tentative claim for a still earlier megaron in the late chalcolithic level XXIV at Beycesultan. Cuyler-Young on the other hand, would not accept either of these buildings at Beycesultan as true megara, and insists that on his narrower definition the first megaron does not appear at Beycesultan until EB. III. He makes a convincing case for the transmission eastwards of the plan from the North West coastal plain of Anatolia at the end of EB. II. In neither of these schemes is any evidence put forward to suggest an Eastern, *i.e.* North Syrian origin for the plan and on present evidence the examples from T. Chuera should be regarded as Anatolian inspired,[4] and post Troy I. Particularly interesting is the apparent fusion of influences to be seen in the Western and Southern temples of Gawra VIIIc where the classic tripartite temple plan known from earlier examples (such as the temple of Level XVIII at Gawra, through the elaborately buttressed example of Level XIII, where the tripartite plan is already undergoing modification) is apparently fused with the Megaron plan, to form what is essentially a tripartite temple with the side aisles extended to form the typical deep porch of the Megaron.[4] This derived plan does not outlive Level VIII at Gawra. The tripartite element then dies out and the true Megaron plan is found at T. Chuera where the Megaron temples appear to last into the second millennium. In Anatolia the plan has a much longer life and reappears in an 8th century context at Gordium.

The second type which appears to be typically Northern is our type H, christened the Flanked Altar plan, where the altar placed on the short wall of a rectangular cella is flanked, either by two niches, or in the later periods by two small rooms. This plan again may ultimately owe its origin to the Tripartite temple, where the central portion of the building frequently exhibits the admittedly not very distinctive features listed above. The study of this type in Chapter III provides an interesting chain of development where some degree of sophistication is added to a basic plan without any fundamental modifications in ritual being indicated. The last example quoted of this genre is the second millennium Dagan temple at Mari, another indication if one is needed of the essential continuity of religious life in the third millennium.

Returning now to the types which both areas have in common. Type A represents the Tripartite Plan of which so much mention has already been made. This plan for long regarded as specifically "Sumerian"[5] appears only in the earliest part of the third millennium and then seems to die out except at T. Gawra where its apparent fusion with the Megaron buys it a little extra time. It seems an improbable contradiction that the "Sumerian" tripartite plan should not survive into the period when Sumerian culture reached its apogee, and underlines forcibly the dangers of attributing linguistic labels to archaeological remains. Its absence in the later Early Dynastic period makes it clear that we ought no longer to refer to the Tripartite Plan as being "Sumerian". In the South, the Jemdet Nasr levels of the Sin temple at Khafaje, *i.e.* Sin I–V are based on the tripartite plan and we can trace the gradual transformation of this plan into the House plan temple of Sin VI of Early Dynastic I. The steps towards this are marked by the progressive development of the courtyard and service rooms until they are all consolidated into one unit which basically resembles that of the ordinary house plan with the cella taking the place of the main reception room.

The only example of Type A from the North is provided by the Eye Temple at T. Braq. Here again the plan is past its grandiose floruit and appears to be part of a larger complex to which it is connected by a series of long narrow storage rooms which flank the west side of the cella. Unfortunately the remains of the Early Dynastic building are too fragmentary to allow us to make any comment on their plan. To sum up, we can say with some degree of certainty that the tripartite plan does not survive after Early Dynastic I and it is only in somewhat peripheral areas, the Diyala and the Khabur, that it survives until Early Dynastic I. The fact that this plan is not known from the Early Dynastic II/Early Dynastic III period at all must mean that this type of building can no longer be labelled as typically Sumerian, though further excavations may cause this statement to be modified. On the other hand a case can be put forward for deriving the House Plan temples and possibly even the Flanked Altar temples from the Tripartite temples of the fourth millennium, thus underlining once more the essential cultural continuity in Iraq despite fluctuations in the composition of the population.

Next we come to Type B, the Single Shrine temple. In a sense this is such a basic plan, a simple rectangle, that it seems unnecessarily pedantic to even list is as a type. As one would expect from such a plan there are a number of examples from the South which cover the whole of the third millennium, but surprisingly only one example from the North, a shrine of uncertain date from T. Chuera, which may not fall within the third millennium at all. The Chuera example has the benches or shelves running round the inside, which so many of the third millennium shrines have to accommodate votive statues, but lacks the buttressing which often dignifies the religious buildings of this period. The fact that it lay below a layer of Nuzi ware and seems to bear no relation to the third millennium Northern Ante Temple which lies to the north-east also suggests an early second rather than a third millennium date. In this case we are left with a third type of shrine which does not appear in the North, a state of affairs which considering the simple nature of the plan probably reflects excavational accident rather than actual fact. These shrines which include the Small, Nintu and Single Shrine temples from Khafaje, the Single Shrine Abu temple from T. Asmar and one of the chapels from the Inanna Temple at Nippur, have the bent axis approach while one, the Jemdet Nasr chapel at Uquair has a direct axis approach. This is in fact chronologically the last appearance of this approach in this category of plan, as the T. Chuera shrine has the Bent Axis approach. Too much chronological significance cannot be read into this, although the direct axis approach does appear to have gone out of fashion by Early Dynastic I, only to be revived again the the Neo-Sumerian period. It is of course to be found earlier in some of the Tripartite temples often in conjunction with a bent axis one. Once again we have failed to "compare and contrast" as the material from the North is so scanty and ill-dated. However with the next group of temples, Group D, the House Plan temples, the situation is improved, the evidence is more abundant and better dated.

In the South we have House Plan temples from the Early Dynastic I levels of the Sin Temple at Khafaje which persist throughout the Early Dynastic, and from the Early Dynastic II Abu or Square temple at T. Asmar. This temple may well be the formalisation of a House Plan temple which dates back to the Archaic shrine. This earlier shrine is not in fact a self-contained unit, but part of something larger, possibly a less geometric attempt at a House Plan temple. In the North we have the Ninni-zaza and Ishtarat temples from Mari and with less certainty the H and G temples at Assur which also represent part of a larger unit, and which appear to centre round a courtyard and to resemble in outline the House Plan temples. In particular the long narrow "Door-room" or hall of Ishtar temple G closely resembles those found in the houses of the "Artisan quarter" at T. Chuera;[6] this feature is not known in the South. The building of a temple planned like an ordinary dwelling house seems a logical step when the city god appears to have been treated as a living force in the running of the town, who had to be provided for in much the same way as the actual human ruler. All these temples are built round a central room which here seems very unlikely to have been roofed as the span is so large. The temple of Ninni-zaza shows two unusual features, one is the elaborate recessed and niched decoration of the walls of the courtyard, and the second is the presence in the centre of the court of a monolith or obelisk. Niched and recessed decoration is not known from the interior of buildings in the South although the same decoration is found on the walls of the courtyard of the Enceinte Sacrée of the Mari Palace. In the South such decoration seems to have been confined to the exterior of the buildings and the obelisk or stele is completely without parallel in the South.[7] Apart from these features the temples basically resemble all the other house plans of the period with a big living room or cella taking up one side of the courtyard. At Khafaje the Sin X temple is unusual in having three parallel rooms which raised certain problems about lighting, and which cannot be paralleled elsewhere in the domestic architecture.[8] The rest of the rooms provide living accommodation and service areas. The presence of stairs in Sin VIII suggests that the flat roof provided further living accommodation as it does today in similar houses. Stairs are not always present, or at least not always discernible, in which case access to the roof may have been by ladder. One recalls the ladder leaning against the wall of the building represented on the "Cult Wagon" from Khafaje. A second storey over part at least of the building is also a possibility.

The House Plan temples have a considerable lifespan although once again evidence from the Agade period is minimal. The mortuary chapels of the Third Ur dynasty are still modelled on this same plan. Here the chapels seem to have been thought of as the living quarters of the dead deified king[9] and the Enceinte Sacrée was rebuilt after the Early Dynastic period although the date of its reconstruction is uncertain. (As mentioned before, the Enceinte is a temple of our Type D).

In type D, the House Plan temples, we have a group of temples closely related to each other, one in the North at Assur, two further south at Mari and one from the Diyala, admittedly all geographically peripheral to the main development of Sumerian culture. We have the dedications for each of these temples, each of which was dedicated to a different divinity three of whom were female and two male so that unlike the Temple Ovals this plan was not "sex linked". Here for the first time in our survey we have a plan of sufficient complexity for its appearance in both our areas to have some possible significance. Moortgat has suggested that this plan had a Western origin, but as we can tentatively trace its development from the Tripartite temple plan at Khafaje and as there are so many parallels in domestic architecture in Mesopotamia it seems unnecessary to look for an alien origin. Here then for the first time we have convincing evidence of cultural interchange and as the development of the plan takes place earlier in the South, we suggest that the North was influenced by the more sophisticated South.

The final group of temples, Group F, presents something of a taxonomic problem, for almost the only feature that the temples have in common is that they are part of a much larger complex. At T. Agrab the complex which contains the Shara Temple is claimed as a religious one, but as sections of the plan are pure reconstruction and we have parallels elsewhere for religious units within administrative buildings, this is open to question. The plan of the shrine itself is also difficult to categorise and really fits none of our types. In some ways it most nearly resembles the Tripartite temples although at Shara one of the aisles has been truncated. It seems highly possible that this "temple" is the sacred area of an administrative building exactly comparable to the palace at Mari with its Enceinte Sacrée. The palace at Mari is undoubtedly a more extensive and more complex building, but then Mari was a much more important centre than T. Agrab. The Enceinte Sacrée itself falls within our type D, the House Plan temples. A second possible member of this category F, is the early temple of Dagan at Mari which is only partially excavated and poorly understood. Parrot claims that the actual sanctuary has not been found and probably lies under the present ziggurat. A series of courts were found and one of them "P" might be interpreted as a Single Shrine temple, but on the published plan of the building there is no trace of an altar although there appears to be a bench or raised platform on two walls. It seems that in these shrines we have an illustration of the thesis mentioned in an earlier chapter that religious and secular matters were not nearly as clearly defined and separated as they are in our present day society, and that we may have been guilty of using an anachronistic "model" in our attempts at interpretation of these remains.

It is interesting to observe that the ziggurat, which even in the third millennium seems to have been an important religious focus in the South, is only found in the North at Mari which it is becoming increasingly clear was culturally more closely linked with the South than with the North or West. The absence of the ziggurat at other Northern sites indicates a considerable difference in religious practise. Moortgat has claimed that the stone buildings, three in all, christened by him Steinbau I, II and III at T. Chuera were stone ziggurats, but until more is understood about their plan and purpose we must tread circumspectly. At the moment the evidence does not appear to warrant this statement. It is by no means certain that the interiors of these constructions were not divided up into rooms, nor is there the slightest evidence for more than one stage on any of them although a finely built flight of stairs was uncovered against the side of Steinbau III.[10] The discovery at T. Braq that the Eye Temples stood on a high platform formed partially of the foundations of earlier temples on the site indicates ties with southern theology, but at Braq again we are dealing with a site like Mari which obviously had a special relationship of some kind with the South.[11] What this special relationship was, it is difficult for us to deduce. There is a case to be made for Mari being another of the city states which emerged in the Early Dynastic period, on equal terms with Kish and Ur and fully within the Sumerian cultural sphere. Braq is a different case, geographically and politically it was a trading post.

This completes our survey of the religious architecture of the two regions and we can tentatively say that while the two areas seem similar in the role assigned to the town god, and the variety of plan, indicating a number of localised cults, there are certain notable differences. The most obvious of these is the absence of the ziggurat in the North; we would be better equipped to deduce the significance of this fact if the function of the ziggurat itself was more clearly understood. One fairly obvious deduction is that the North excluding Mari was poorer both in manpower and actual wealth and might have found such a massive investment of labour and resources beyond its scope. This deduction is upheld by several other features. The elaboration of multiple shrines such as is achieved in even such a comparatively provincial centre as Khafaje, and the wealth of ornamentation like that on the temple at Al Ubaid, is nowhere duplicated in the smaller temples of the North. It does seem to indicate that the South had a more evolved and sophisticated philosophy, as well as greater material wealth, a fact which is perhaps also suggested by the elaboration of the burial rite in the South. Such an elaboration of ritual as is witnessed in the Royal Graves at Ur is only necessary if a fairly sophisticated picture of life after death has been built up.

If we look at the distribution in time of the temple plans, the most striking feature is the longevity of some of them. Type B is so simple that it is not surprising to find examples at every period in the third millennium; type C as mentioned before is presumed to occur throughout the same period although examples are only known for the beginning of the millennium, from Nippur, and from the end of it at Ur. Type H, from the North, is again a relatively simple plan which probably derives from the fourth millennium and is certainly attested into the second. Two types which first occur in Early Dynastic I/II are types D and F both of which flourish well into the second millennium. The only two at the moment which appear to be useful as dating criteria are types A, Tripartite and E, Oval; type A because it does not occur after the Jemdet Nasr and type E because it seems to be confined in time to Early Dynastic II/III with a slight overlap into the early Agade period.

Attempts have been made in the past to deduce changes and

developments in theologies from the changes in the plans of religious buildings. The comment which is usually made on the third millennium is that it is the period when man was cut off from direct contact with his god and might only approach him through the intermediary of a priest. This is symbolised by the growing inaccessibility of the cella and the enclosing of the shrine and service rooms in an outer wall. This interpretation appears a little naive when it is remembered that this period also saw the introduction of shrines in private houses and the development of the idea of a personal god. In some ways the relationship of the gods to men became more exactly defined; the god ruled the town, lived in a house like his human deputy, and his wants were ministered to in the same ways. If the presence of House Plan temples does indeed indicate this then we can say that the idea of theocratic rule was held in the North as well as the South.

Turning now to the non-religious building it is interesting to attempt to make sociological and economic deductions, albeit of a generalised nature. We have seen that so-called palaces are found throughout the third millennium in the South. It is only fair to say that the status of the Jemdet Nasr palace, the earliest example, is in considerable doubt and were it not for the apparent existence of secular public buildings as early as the Ubaid period one would be tempted to class it as a religious building.[12] The first undeniably administrative building is the Kish A palace and the structure of these palaces, comprising as we have said before several suites of rooms bound into a unit by a heavy outer wall, serves to underline the multiple tasks falling to the administrators of the period. This tradition of planning continues into the Ur III period where the plan of the Giparu at Ur with its insulating corridor running round three sides of the building and the interior divided by another passage into two separate units obviously with different functions, is in exactly the same tradition. As one would expect from the evidence of the temples indicating poorer communities, the North, with the exception of Mari and Braq whose special relationship with the South has already been mentioned, has no buildings of comparable complexity. The complex at T. Gawra consisting of barrel-vaulted hall and modest adjacent living quarters suggests a more patriarchal governmental system, similar perhaps to that of the Arab tribes of the Southern Marshes today, with the barrel-vaulted chamber filling the same role as the reed Mudhifs of the South. At T. Taya too there is evidence for at least one house of some importance on the citadel, and its position, protected by the elaborate citadel wall, would suggest that this too was the home of a local headman.

Although we have seen that the North appears to have been less prosperous than the South, both areas found it necessary to build defensive walls presumably as protection against their neighbours and also, if one applies a modern analogy, as protection against the nomadic bands from the Western desert and from the Eastern Highlands. The invasions of the Lullubi and the Ummanmanda were probably the culmination of a long tradition of piratical raids. Certainly we have evidence for their incursions as early as the reign of Naram-Sin.[13]

Evidence of some degree of town planning, a further indication of centralised control, has been quoted from both areas and the larger scale of the undertakings in the South leads one to deduce a greater amount of bureaucratic control, an impression borne out by the infinitely greater amount of inscribed material, much of it administrative in content, from the South. Many of these tablets are loosely described as economic and the presence of the industrial area at Uruk as early as the Jemdet Nasr period, of the possible fish processing area at Tello and of the probably industrial building known as the Northern palace at T. Asmar, all suggest a more highly developed economic system in the South than in the North. There is no comparable evidence from the North although a flint-knapping area was found at T. Taya. The South as pointed out elsewhere[14] is dependent on imports for even the most basic commodities such as hard timber and stone, and therefore was almost forced into developing a thriving import/export trade for which we have textual evidence from as early as the time of Ur-Nanse of Lagash.[15] Excavations in the South have produced far greater wealth of imported material ranging from carnelian, steatite, lapis-lazuli, obsidian and sea-shells to both base and precious metals. The North is poorer both in scope and quantity of imports. There can be no doubt that the South possessed a more developed economy and quite possibly a more developed epigraphic and numerical system with which to service it, as well as a more powerful bureaucracy.

When we attempt to compare the domestic architecture of North and South we are at once confronted with the familiar problems. The North has produced very little domestic architecture, the only house plans coming from Gawra in Level VI, T. Taya and from possibly T. Chuera. Mari once again shows such Southern affinities that it seems anomalous to class her as "Northern". The evidence from Gawra is unrewarding in that, in many cases, the foundations alone were recovered with no internal doors, so that the limits of each house are impossible to determine. The buildings are not detached. All one can say with some degree of certainty is that the plan at Gawra is quite unlike the courtyard house of the South, the plan is rectilinear, there is no conclusive evidence for a second floor but it is highly likely that one was present, and it is impossible to tell for certain whether there is a big difference in the range of area covered by each house. The rooms are small with few distinguishing features although a substantially built group of rooms in square J.7[16] may have belonged to a larger unit. It is interesting to note that there are no public or religious buildings in Level VI at T. Gawra except the presumed gatehouses and watchtower, in sharp contrast to the position in Level VIII. One is tempted to suggest that the town was taken over by entirely new people in Level VI. This hypothesis is supported by a break in the typology of the pottery[17] which must at least represent a considerable cultural upheaval. Level VIII was destroyed by fire, as was Level VI, further indications of unsettled times. The houses at T. Taya show some Southern features but others such as the cellars with rock cut tombs are unknown elsewhere.

Once again the evidence from T. Chuera must be treated with some caution. The first problem is to determine whether the buildings in fact represent houses or whether they are, as has been suggested, an elaborate series of mortuary chapels. Until their association with graves of consequence can be satisfactorily demonstrated the present author prefers to regard them as houses with domestic chapels, a phenomenon which as it has been shown may have occurred at Khafaje and T. Asmar at about the same period. The long narrow "door room" is a feature not found in the South but which is present in the House Plan temple of Assur G. If these rooms are regarded as houses the three complete plans excavated show considerable variation in size from seven to nine, or possibly ten rooms each, which would agree well with evidence from the South. In the South this led us to deduce a considerable social and financial inequality among the inhabitants of the houses.

Obviously it would be rash to make such a claim for the North on the strength of three house plans from an insecurely dated level at a peripheral site, but the suggestion that there was a certain class or wealth stratification in the North is strengthened by the discovery of the "Headman's" house in Gawra VIIIA. Such a building must, as has already been suggested, point to a certain focusing of authority and a certain social stratification even if it was only the paternalism exercised by many Arab sheiks today. The fact that only a small proportion of the population was buried on the acropolis at Gawra, and a smaller proportion still was buried in tombs, rather than graves, again points to some sort of discrimination plausibly based on a social hierarchy.[18] The discovery of the interesting burial complex at T. Chuera has been interpreted by the excavator as a royal burial in which the main bodies, probably those of a man and a woman, were accompanied by a number of "soldiers" forming a bodyguard. If this interpretation is broadly correct then here again we have striking evidence of a hierarchical society.

Finally we come to the puzzle presented by the circular house models from Mari. We have said repeatedly that Mari is culturally closer to the South than the North, but in this instance the only parallels in Mesopotamia for these models come from the earlier Round House of T. Gawra. There is nothing comparable known from the South. Even if the comparison with the Round House is a valid one the location of one of the models below a road in the Early Dynastic town at Mari remains a mystery. Is it possible that these models, stocked perhaps with food and drink in the vessels found inside one of them, were regarded as refuges for the spirits of the town in times of trouble? It has been suggested that the function of the real round houses was to serve as refuges. A feature which perhaps tells against this interpretation is the large and apparently unfortified, unprotected entrance on the Mari models. If however beasts had to be herded into these buildings for safety a large entrance would have been necessary. It is of course also possible that these models represent some sort of mythological dwelling rather than an earthly one. It does seem possible that some sort of circular house survived in the North after what is at present its last archaeologically attested appearance in Gawra XI.

Surveying all the evidence we can come as we hoped to certain tentative sociological conclusions; it has been accepted for some time now that economically the South had outstripped the North by the third millennium and all the evidence confirms this. In the South the population was larger, the first city had appeared followed by others, the standard of living was higher with a greater differentiation between rich and poor and a more hierarchical social order existed. Although technologically North and South appear to have reached similar levels of achievement, except perhaps in metallurgy, the South shows a greater artistic sophistication, and also it would appear from the complexity of some of the temple plans a greater sophistication in thought. Both texts and archaeological remains bear witness to the increasing number of functionaries attached to the palace and the temple. From the evidence of the "palaces" a more elaborate system of government can be deduced. On the other hand there is no evidence from the North for anything other than a patriarchal system of government. Both areas seem to show the lack of a national religion, reflecting perhaps the lack of a strong centralising government. If the evidence were available it would be interesting to see whether the temple plans of the Agade period, when a strong central government existed for almost the first time, showed less variety and more standardisation. The pains taken by Sargon and Naram-Sin to placate the local gods wherever they went suggest that no conscious attempt was made to impose a state religion, unless the deification of Naram-Sin was a step in this direction. The sack and desecration of Nippur was such an atypical event that it was immortalized in "The Curse of Akkad". The only convincing explanation would seem to be that it was a political expedient perhaps necessitated by the revolt of Nippur against the secular might of Naram-Sin rather than a deliberate attempt to undermine the Sumerian religion.

It is very difficult to assess the amount of contact that there was between the two areas. There must inevitably have been a good deal of through traffic, but the architectural evidence rather seems to suggest that apart from one or two well established staging posts on important trade routes such as T. Braq and perhaps T. Chuera,[19] the Southerners had very little contact with, or effect on, the people of the North except in most general terms. The exception to this is of course Mari which as we have already suggested was culturally almost entirely within the southern sphere of influence. For example Mari is at the moment the most northerly site at which evidence of the Persian Gulf trade as witnessed by the steatite hut pots, is found.[20] On the other hand, a certain amount of western influence is suggested at this site by the obelisk in the Ninna-zaza temple. By and large, excluding that particular feature there is nothing in the architecture of Mari which would be out of place at Ur, or Khafaje, or any other southern centre. The other Western trait found in the architecture of the North is of course, the Megaron, almost certainly an instance of cultural borrowing. The South shows very little evidence of outside influence in its architecture; there is plenty of evidence for foreign contacts in the form of imported materials, but there is no one characteristic to which one can point as having originated outside Mesopotamia. This leads one to suggest that in the third millennium Southern Iraq was architecturally ahead of its neighbours, including North Mesopotamia, and so had no impetus to borrow from them.[21] The apparent lack of contacts between North and South is one of the more surprising features, the only architectural evidence of direct borrowing seems to be provided by the House Plan temples in the North. As the plan is known earlier in the South, and as the domestic buildings of similar plan seem to be native to the South, it is reasonable to suggest that the examples in the North are borrowed from the South. The fact North and South followed their own lines of development perhaps underlines among other things, the physical dichotomy of the two areas; the Jazirah has its geographic links primarily with the West, and to a certain extent to the North East, while Southern Iraq tends, geographically towards the South and South East. The Euphrates is a potentially excellent North-South corridor which does not seem to have been fully exploited at this period.

In order even to attempt to write an economic and social history of the third millennium new evidence is imperative. Two needs stand out as paramount. Perhaps the most important is for an intensive survey of the North in order to enlarge our scanty knowledge of the settlement patterns in this area. Such surveys may alter many of our present assumptions as to the conditions prevailing in the Jazirah and indeed may show that the greater sophistication in the South is more imagined than real. The second requirement is extensive survey and excavation of a considerable area of a large town site in order to give us a cross section illustrating the industrial and social life of the period. We desperately need this evidence if we are to make any but the most banal generalizations on these aspects of life in Mesopotamia. We also need evidence from a number of small rural communities to round out the picture and to balance our view. In terms of artefacts such evidence is not likely to add greatly to our picture of the material culture as most town dwellers were still basically agriculturalists, nor is it likely to provide further art objects. The excavation of a large corpus of skeletal material would give us valuable evidence on dietetics, diseases and life expectancy.

If this survey, by collecting all the available material on one topic, has highlighted the deficiencies in the evidence and pointed the way for further research, then it has achieved something worthwhile.

NOTES

[1]   A.Tobler, *T. Gawra* II, p. 72. Herring bone wall is attributed to L.XI and is part of tomb G.36.104. Tobler feels that the peculiar method of laying the brick is dictated by the shape of the tomb.

[2]   Cf. Chapter III for the house at T. Taya and Chapter IV for the Nuzi models.

[3] A.Moortgat, *Art of Ancient Mesopotamia*, p. 58.

[4] For a survey of the architecture from T. Gawra, cf. A.L.Perkins. *Comparative Stratigraphy*, p. 65—70 and p. 172—177; also *B.Hrouda*, 'Die "Megaron" Bauten', in Vorderasien. *Anadolu* XIV, p. 1—14; T.Cuyler-Young, 'The Architecture of Hasanlu' IV. *Iranica Antiqua* 6, esp. p. 66 ff.

[5] T.B.Jones, The Sumerian problem, particularly phase III, p. 104.

[6] For the door-room of the Ishtar temple, W.Andrae, *Das Weiderstandene Assur*, p. 73, Abb. 33, and for T. Chuera, Moortgat, *Ist campaign*, Abb. 32, p. 34 and *2nd campaign*, plan II "Hauser".

[7] A.Parrot in *M.A.M.* III, p. 26, points out the obelisk is a feature previously thought to be confined to Canaan and Phoenica; the Mari example is also considerably earlier than most of the comparable examples from the West.

[8] The fragment of a house plan found on a clay tablet at Nippur may perhaps show three parallel rooms, cf. McCown and Haines, *Nippur I*, pl. 52a and b.

[9] Moortgat, *Art of Mesopotamia*, p. 60—61 and pl. 46.

[10] A.Moortgat, *T. Chuera, 5th campaign*, pp. 4—7.

[11] This relationship is most clearly demonstrated by the remains of the latest Eye temple at T. Braq which both in plan and proportions has obvious close affinities with the south. Prof. Mallowan has pointed out the significant 3:1 ratio in the plan of the cella at Braq, at Warka and at Uquair, *C.A.H.* I, pt. 2, p. 247.

[12] The type of "zingel" wall found at Jemdet Nasr usually associated with temples and the administrative buildings, as we have shown in Chapter II, tend to be distinguished by a passage running round inside a single external wall. For a public building of the Ubaid period at T. Uquair, cf. J.N.E.S. II.2, p. 137, and pl. VIb.

[13] For instance the stele of Naram-sin mentions a campaign against the Lullubi and the rock carvings of Darband-i-Gawr bear witness to his activities in the N-E as does a macehead now in the British Museum from Luristan dedicated by Naram-Sin to the god Aba.

[14] H.E.W.Crawford in *Man, Settlement and Urbanism*, ed. Ucko *et al.*, p. 761.

[15] Sollberger and Kupper, *Inscriptions Royales*, no. Ic3e, p. 46.

[16] E.A.Speiser, *T. Gawra* I, pl. VII and pp. 18—21.

[17] E.A.Speiser, *op. cit.*, p. 49.

[18] Other explanations such as the practise of differing rites like cremation or exposure might also be used to explain the discrepancy. It should also be noted that 80% of the burials were infants or children which perhaps

indicates discrimination on doctrinal grounds rather than on those of social status. On the other hand in a cemetery at Ubaid excavated by H.Wright, all the 28 graves dug were those of men of similar age and wealth suggesting a sex discrimination.

[19] For a concise description of the trade routes, cf. D.Oates, *Studies in the Ancient History of Northern Iraq*, pp. 5—8. It is interesting to speculate on the possibility of the existence of Karums in foreign countries even as early as this. Possibly further excavations at T. Chuera may throw light on this.

[20] A curious steatite fragment of a so-called kohl pot with a gabled building scratched on it comes from Gawra XII, but is in a completely different style; cf. A.Tobler, T. Gawra II, p. 208 and pl. XCV.d.

[21] It is always possible that this impression is erroneous and due to the lack of excavated material in neighbouring countries rather than to the postulated superiority of Sumer. It seems highly likely that further excavations in Iran will cause this long-established view to be drastically modified.

TEMPLE TYPES — South

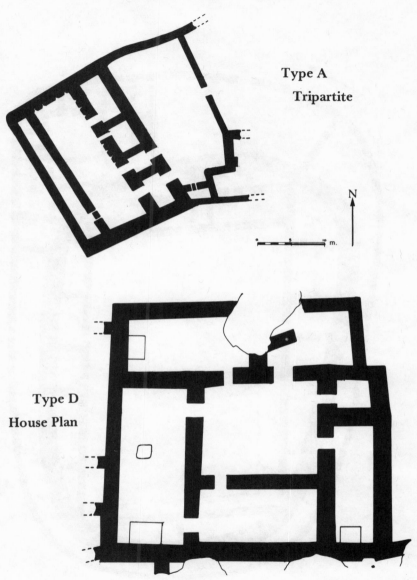

Type A
Tripartite

N

Type D
House Plan

Fig. 1

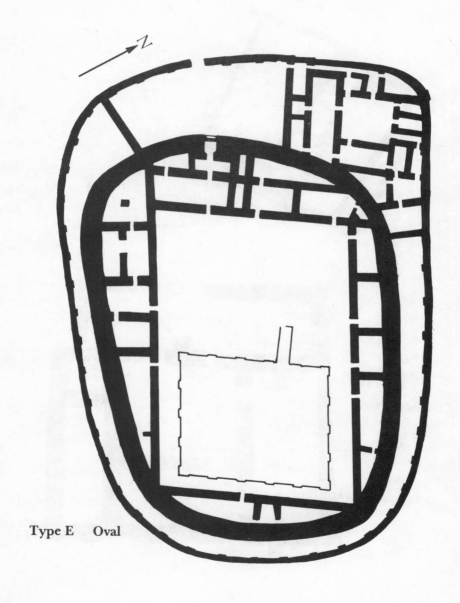

Type E   Oval

Fig. 2

HOUSE TYPES — South

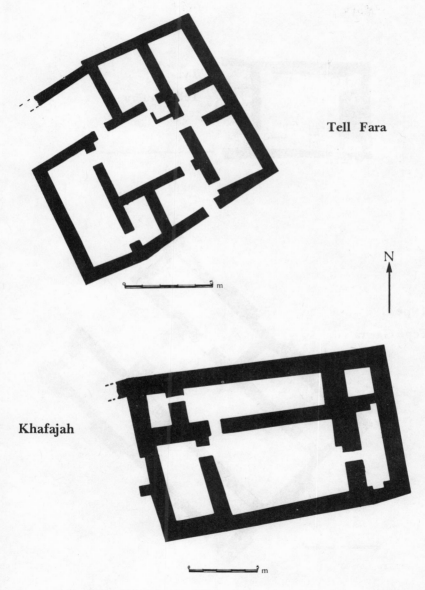

Tell Fara

Khafajah

N

Fig. 3

TEMPLE TYPES — North

"Megaron"

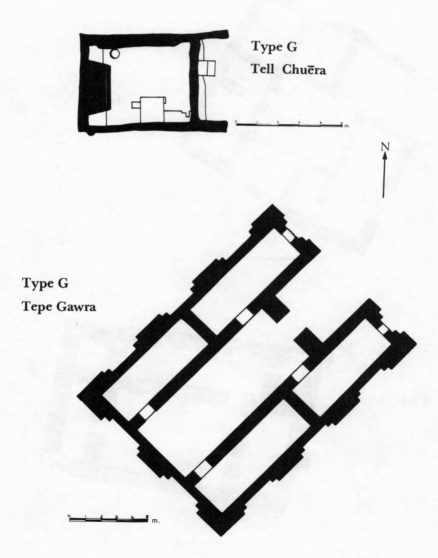

Type G
Tell Chuēra

Type G
Tepe Gawra

N

Fig. 4

DEVELOPMENT OF FLANKED ALTAR PLAN

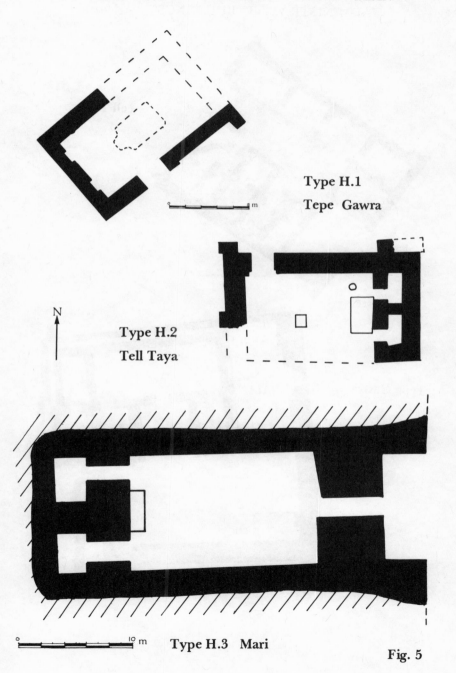

Type H.1
Tepe Gawra

N

Type H.2
Tell Taya

Type H.3   Mari

Fig. 5

PRIVATE HOUSE and
"ADMINISTRATIVE BUILDINGS" – North

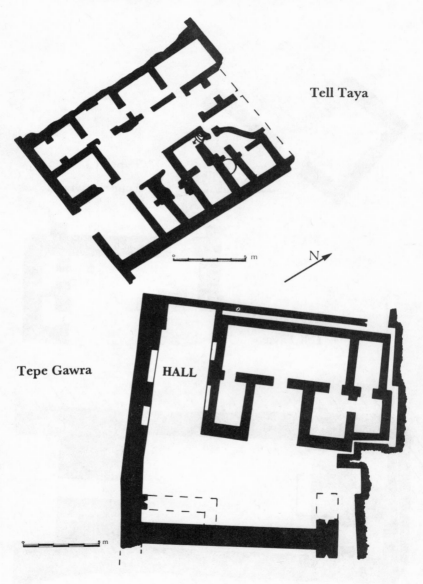

Tell Taya

N

Tepe Gawra

HALL

Fig. 6

INDEX